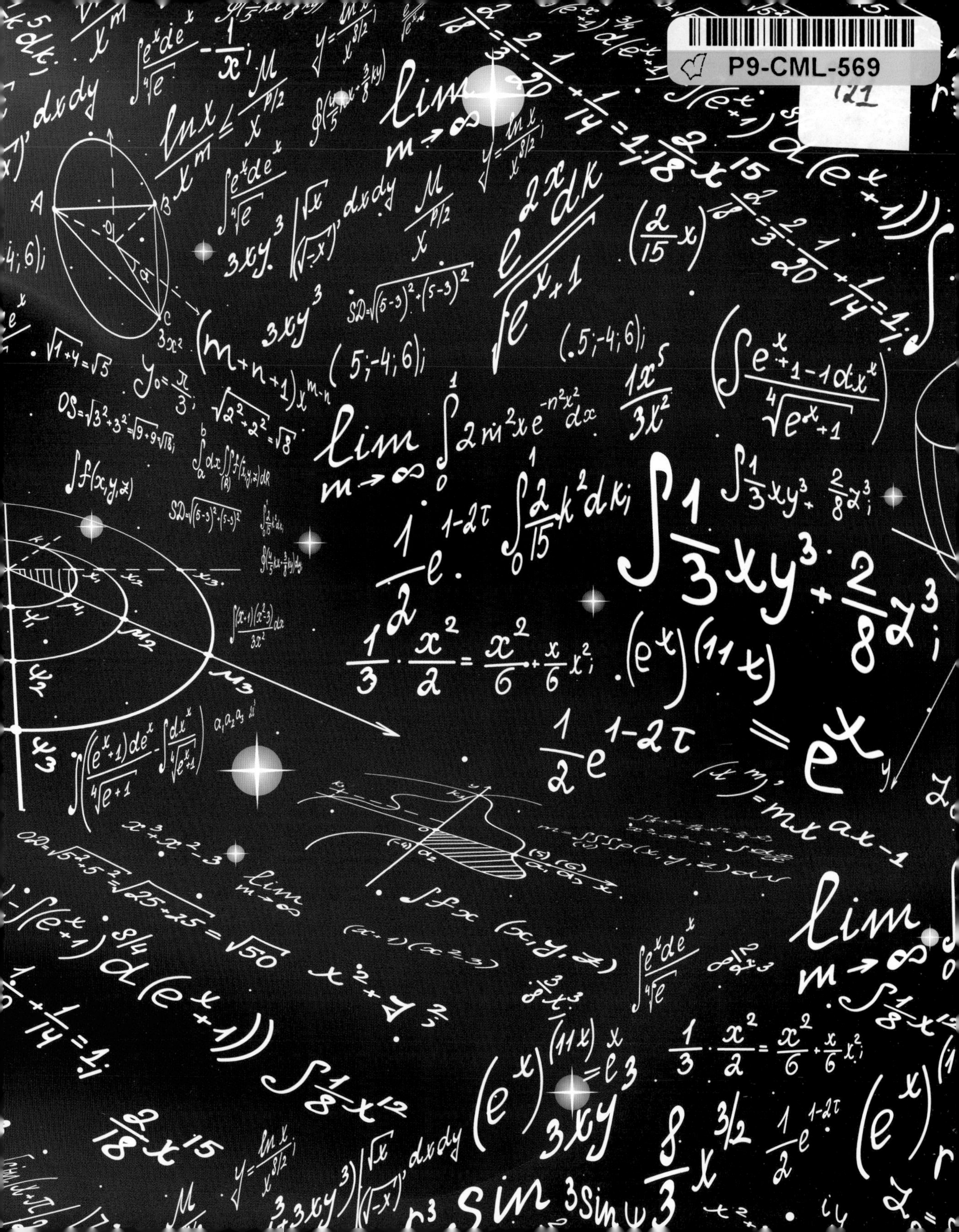

WONDER WOMEN OF SCIENCE

Twelve Geniuses Who Are Currently Rocking
Science, Technology, and the World

TIERA FLETCHER
AND GINGER RUE
ILLUSTRATED BY SALLY WERN COMPORT

CANDLEWICK PRESS

First edition 2021

Library of Congress Catalog Card Number pending
ISBN 978-1-5362-0734-7

20 21 22 23 24 25 TLF 10 9 8 7 6 5 4 3 2 1

Printed in Dongguan, Guangdong, China

This book was typeset in Droid Serif.

Candlewick Press
99 Dover Street
Somerville, Massachusetts 02144

www.candlewick.com

To my husband, Myron Sr. Thank you for your love, inspiration, and dedication to uplifting me at all times.

To my sons, Myron Jr. and Micah, for being my motivation and the first lines of my legacy.

To my parents, Emery and Sheila Guinn. Special thanks for the years of sacrifice, support, and unconditional love.

To my nieces, Kamora, Kayla, and Tahiry. Special thanks for your dreams and aspirations to secure the future of female empowerment.

To my sister and brother for their tough love and unwavering support.

TF

For Dwight and Pearson, my in-house engineers

GR

CONTENTS

TIERA FLETCHER

[**FACT FILE**

HOMETOWN: Mableton, GA

EDUCATION: BS in Aerospace, Aeronautical, and Astronautical Engineering, Massachusetts Institute of Technology (2017)

EMPLOYMENT: Aerospace Engineer, working on NASA's Space Launch System, which will power humans to Mars and beyond

TOP HONORS AND ACHIEVEMENTS: *Good Housekeeping* Magazine's Awesome Women Award (2017); National Society of Black Engineers 21st Century Trailblazers in Human Spaceflight Award (2018); Most Promising Engineer in Industry, Black Engineer of the Year Awards (2019)

Our deepest fear is not that we are inadequate. Our deepest fear is that we are powerful beyond measure." I spoke these words by author Marianne Williamson at my eighth-grade graduation ceremony, and I think about them every day.

When I had to recite that passage before delivering the speech

in front of my peers, I realized how much I had been living in fear. My science teacher would always describe me as the one who was super smart—but not initially, obviously so. I was the shy kid in the class. Even if I knew the answer, I was afraid to speak up because I did not have the confidence to showcase my abilities.

I was six when I started preparing for my career as an engineer. On our Saturday trips to the grocery store, my mother, an accountant, would tell me to total up the cost of groceries, plus sales tax and minus the coupons I'd clipped the night before. Of course, there was no calculator . . . I *was* the calculator! Math became a fun challenge for me, and at the same time, I was beginning to understand one of math's uses: managing money. My father, a construction worker, must have noticed my interest because soon enough he taught me how to calculate measurements when building a structure. I guess being the child of an accountant and a construction worker may explain why I wanted to be a mathematician, architect, scientist, inventor, *and* designer . . . at least until my next big realization.

At the age of eleven, I discovered the name of my future career field: aerospace engineering. Growing up in a small town called Mableton, Georgia, I was a short distance from Lockheed Martin in Marietta, Georgia. Lockheed Martin created a program that allowed select elementary school students to learn the fundamentals of aerospace engineering. When I was picked for the program, I decided that I wanted to design military aircraft.

From that point on, my academic focus was aerospace

engineering. I knew that I had to excel to be a rocket scientist, so I became my own worst critic. Meanwhile, my family continued to be my cheerleaders.

You might say I was afraid not of the dark, but of the light—the light inside myself. No matter how many perfect grades I received, I did not believe in my abilities. Even though I went on to major in aerospace engineering at the Massachusetts Institute of Technology (MIT), one of the top engineering schools in the entire world, I did not believe in myself.

Within the first month of college, I lost one of my closest friends to suicide. He faced many pressures in his young life, including both his father and his older brother going to jail. While living at home with his single mom, he tried his best to help out by working two jobs in addition to his full-time college studies. Eventually, he became lost and overwhelmed. Our family lives were different, but our self-doubt was the same. My friend did not see in himself the capable, strong, gifted person I knew him to be. Like me, he simply did not believe in himself. After his tragic and untimely death, I made a commitment to carry the faith that he had in me and achieve my dreams like he knew I could.

It was then I realized that life is too short to make excuses and to not at least try to reach your full potential. As you know, that is much easier said than done. I consistently fought to prove myself in classes with few

female or minority students. To this day, there are not many people who look like me in my line of work. I have felt underrepresented and frustrated many times. I had professors who would comment that my presentation delivery was too feminine even after I received a perfect grade. I quickly learned I had to project my voice to be heard in discussions where I was often the only woman in the group. Many times, my male peers assumed that I would not be able to contribute to a group project simply because I am female. Even in the industry, I run into many people who do not expect me to be able to answer their questions; they incorrectly assume that a woman couldn't possibly have the required knowledge and understanding. As a triple minority in the field of aerospace engineering (young, female, and African American), I have continually experienced false assumptions based on the way that I look. These assumptions have followed me since I first realized I wanted to be an engineer at eleven years old. But do you think I let those assumptions stop me? No way! Every day, it is an uphill battle, but of course, I do not fight alone. I have the unceasing support of my parents, my family, my friends, my mentors, and my husband.

At age twenty-two, I achieved my first career dream: I became a rocket scientist, working on NASA's Space Launch System, and I graduated from MIT with a bachelor of science in aerospace engineering. The following year, I married my best friend, coworker, and life partner, Myron Fletcher, and I gave birth to my motivation, my son, Myron Jr.

As I continue to make a life for myself, I always remember my close friend who so tragically took his own life. His potential and the potential of many others like him had been cut short. To address that issue, my husband and I founded Rocket with the Fletchers, an organization that offers motivational speaking and mentoring services to encourage others to reach their fullest potential and achieve their dreams.

The twelve scientists profiled here are women from all sorts of backgrounds who are currently rocking science, technology, engineering, and mathematics. Each of them has a different story to tell about how she got to where she is today, but the one thing they have in common is that they are all truly wonder women of science. Around the world, there are many more women doing incredible work and breaking new ground in STEM fields—not to mention girls of all ages dreaming of how they will one day contribute.

Perseverance, support, faith, and unwavering diligence are the keys to achieving your dreams. You may not realize it, but at this very moment, you hold these keys in your hand. Now go and use them to unlock your future. Someday you, too, could be a science superstar!

DAVINA DURGANA

Fighting Modern Slavery through Math

[FACT FILE

HOMETOWN: Dix Hills, NY

EDUCATION: BA in International Affairs, The George Washington University (2010); Certificat en Sciences Politiques, Université Panthéon Sorbonne (2012); MA in International Affairs, Conflict Resolution, and Civil Society Development, American University of Paris (2012); PhD in International Relations, American University (2015)

EMPLOYMENT: International Human Rights Statistician and Vice Chair, Statistics without Borders

TOP HONORS AND ACHIEVEMENTS: Trafficking in America Task Force Award for Service (2013); Harry V. Roberts Statistical Advocate of the Year (2016); *Forbes* 30 Under 30 in Science (2017)

Word problems. Love them or hate them, you've probably seen them on tests and homework plenty of times. If a train leaves the station at 6 a.m. traveling 90 mph, and a second train leaves the station at 6:15 a.m. traveling 100 mph, why are the conductors in such a hurry, and how many cups of espresso did they drink that morning in the first place?

OK, that one is pretty meaningless. But for Dr. Davina Durgana, word problems are far from meaningless. They're actually extremely important . . . because her *word* problems are real-life *world* problems.

Durgana is a statistician, which is a type of mathematician who deals with large amounts of data. Statisticians use information we know to try to figure out information we don't know, often by means of extrapolation. Extrapolation is a kind of guessing, but it's not blind guessing, like "Can you guess what kind of animal we're thinking about right now?" (By the way, it's a panda. Awww!)

Let's say you have a warehouse full of boxes of oranges. (Why do you have a warehouse full of oranges? We don't know . . . Maybe you're a really rich person who loves citrus? Maybe you have an extreme fear of vitamin C deficiency? Just stick with us.) You decide you want to know how many oranges you have in total, but it would take you at least two weeks to go through every single box and count every single orange, and by then, the oranges would be rotten. What do you do? Well, since the boxes are all the same size, you take down three boxes (a representative sample) and count the number of oranges in each box. In the first box, there are twenty; in the second, there are twenty-three; and in the third, there are twenty-two. Based on this knowledge, you can extrapolate that in each box in your warehouse, you have about twenty-one or twenty-two oranges (or 21.7 oranges, but 0.7 orange is kind of ridiculously precise). You can then multiply that number by the total number of boxes in the warehouse to figure out how many oranges you have altogether. Congratulations! You've just come up with a statistic!

As you can see, extrapolation is much more precise than guessing games because it doesn't just pull a possible answer out of thin air. Extrapolating is a way of finding an answer we *don't* have by using data we *do* have from similar circumstances. And Davina Durgana figured out how to use extrapolation to try to help solve a global humanitarian crisis.

One of the biggest problems of our time is slavery . . . which is kind of mind-blowing, because many people assume that slavery was a terrible thing that ended many years ago. Maybe we thought (or hoped!) that humankind had outgrown anything so horrific and primitive, but it turns out that there are still people who will do unimaginably bad things to other people for their own personal gain. Durgana defines modern slavery as the exploitation of one person for another person's profit, and today slavery takes the form of forced labor, forced marriage, and forced prostitution. When people are moved around from one place to another for these purposes, it's called human trafficking. And sadly it's such a terrible problem that many people don't even want to think about it.

But lucky for the world, Davina Durgana is so brave that she *does* think about slavery. Like, all the time. And even luckier for the world, Durgana figured out a way to use her mad skills in math to convince other people to think about it, too—which is the first step toward actually stopping slavery.

Here's what she did.

Slavery is a secret thing, obviously, because it's illegal and wrong, and if more people knew about it, they'd try to put a stop to it. So human traffickers work very hard to make sure no one knows what they're doing. If countries could get data—concrete numbers about how many people are enslaved—it would give us a starting point for working on how to stop it because at least then we'd know how big the problem truly is. But nobody thought it would ever be possible to actually get these numbers. You see, even when governments do have some idea of how many people within their borders are enslaved, they don't always want to share this information with other countries . . . because, well, it's not exactly a great way to promote tourism. (Ever seen a "Welcome to ___, Slavery Capital of the World" sign? Neither have we.) So Durgana faces two challenges: first, getting secret numbers no one knows about, and second, getting numbers countries *do* know about but don't want to report.

Once she does get a solid set of numbers, though, Durgana uses it to extrapolate how big the problem actually is. For example, if Country A is like Country B and you have accurate slavery data from Country A, you can extrapolate how much slavery is happening in Country B based on the numbers you have from Country A. And once you have these numbers, you can use them to get the attention of powerful people who can help do something about it.

While the numbers are important, Durgana also works to get specific true stories from the people those numbers represent—because stories, not numbers, connect human beings together. These two types of data are called quantitative (numbers) and qualitative (stories). (For more info on the difference between quantitative and qualitative research and why they're both useful, check out the feature on page 18.)

Now that, like us, you're thoroughly impressed with Durgana, let's find out a little more about how she wound up taking on some of the scariest villains of our time.

[THE SPARK

Davina grew up in Long Island, New York, in a town called Dix Hills. Her dad was a civil engineer with master's degrees in engineering and business, and her mom was a computer scientist with master's degrees in education and business—and the two of them later started their own telecommunications company. (Davina comes from a family of high achievers, apparently.)

In middle school, Davina was a "bookworm" who "got made fun of all the time," she says. "I was always reading. At family parties . . . in the shower or tub . . . at the dinner table. The punishment my parents used on me was taking away my books!" A longtime member of Girl Scouts, Davina also enjoyed playing volleyball and being on the track team, but never as much as she loved books. The only passion that ever came close to books for her? Rescue dogs. "I'm obsessed with animals," she confesses. "Always have been."

Growing up, Davina and her two younger sisters were very involved in their church's youth group, and that's actually what got Davina interested in the problem of human trafficking. Davina's church group worked with a children's human rights

organization in the country of El Salvador, where Davina traveled on a mission trip when she was a freshman in college. Because Davina was good with languages—she was fluent in French and also spoke Spanish—she acted as the trip translator and also taught math and English. Most of the trip went smoothly. *Most of it.* "My Spanish was far from perfect," Durgana admits. "We got really close to all of the children, and I was trying to tell one of them that my family wanted to sponsor his education. Somehow, I accidentally ended up saying that we wanted to adopt him, and his mom got kind of scared that we were going to just take him away from her and home with us!"

El Salvador was a dangerous place at the time. The Durganas made their family mission trip in 2007, and just the year before, the US State Department's Overseas Security Advisory Council ranked El Salvador as one of the most violent countries in the world, estimating that the country had an average of ten murders per day. When Davina and her family were there, they learned of children being enslaved, and a young child who was the cousin of a child Davina worked with was killed. "I was so upset," Durgana recalls. "I cared so much about the children we worked with, and an El Salvadoran gang was selling these children into slavery, and no one seemed to be able to stop them. I did some research and found out that it was also going on in other places—even in the United States. I came back to Washington, DC, where I was in college at George Washington University, and I interned for every organization in DC that had anything to do with human rights or trafficking and would take me.

"I started hearing stories in the media here and there, and it made me wonder where the information came from. I wondered, who is getting and giving this information? I knew that the funding to fight slavery should be based on the data. I finally decided I would improve these measurements of how big the problem actually is." Before Durgana, very few people had really attempted to tackle the human trafficking problem mathematically in the United States. "It seemed too hard," she explains. "I was told there were too many data gaps, too many privacy concerns, too much to coordinate. People said there was no way anyone could come up with a good enough model to predict vulnerability of children to human trafficking, but I was able to make a strong model out of data that other people had previously thought wasn't useful."

Oddly enough, no one expected Davina to become a statistician. She was so good with languages that everyone—including Davina—expected that to be her thing, even though she'd also always been ridiculously good at math. But Durgana thinks the study of foreign languages and the study of mathematics aren't actually so different. "I saw a lot of patterns and commonalities in language, and I think that helped me see those things in numbers, too," she explains. "So both math and languages feel like pattern recognition to me. Also, math is consistent across cultural boundaries, so knowing math as well as foreign languages is helpful in globally fighting slavery." Durgana credits her foreign-language teachers for much of her work today: "Communicating in French about high-level statistics is fascinating! Communication can be a big barrier and impediment to overcome, so I am thankful that I had great foreign-language teachers."

While studying international relations as an undergraduate and then statistics in her master's and doctoral programs, Davina stayed busy outside the classroom as well. She supported a Girl Scouts troop in DC, worked as a children's advocate in the court system, landed internships on Capitol Hill and in the White House, worked with Big Brothers Big Sisters, and served as an EMT (emergency medical technician). Everything she did made her think more and more about the problem of slavery. "In each capacity, I found ways to integrate these interests into the bigger picture of human trafficking," she explains. "For example, I came up with ways for EMTs and firefighters to recognize human trafficking so they could be on the lookout for victims during their work."

[THE EUREKA MOMENT

Being recognized for her academic accomplishments gave Davina the confidence that she could take on real-life challenges. She took a college entrance exam as a fifth grader, just to see how she'd do, and totally killed it. By the time she was ready to graduate high school, she was both a National Merit Semifinalist and a Talent Search Scholar.

Placing in science and math fairs and in national foreign-language contests also built her confidence, and her teachers often told her parents that Davina was one of the brightest students they'd ever had. "You don't know your accomplishments aren't normal until someone tells you," she explains. This validation made Davina want to try to do hard things no one else ever had, especially when people said it couldn't be done—like getting numerical data on slavery.

And it was her work in El Salvador that made Davina know

she had to devote her life to helping enslaved people. "Realizing people could die was scary to me," she says. "I had never lost anyone close to me, but to have a child die in the community we'd gotten so close to made me realize it could have been any of the kids we'd gotten to know." Davina came to believe that numbers and data were the best way to protect vulnerable people.

[NOTE TO SELF

"If I could tell my younger self anything," Durgana says, "it would be 'Don't be scared to follow your interests.'" For a long time, no one understood what Durgana was trying to do with statistics and slavery. "I would talk about human rights, and people would say, 'What kind of job is that? What are you going to do?' So I'd tell my younger self that you can make a career out of what you love."

She'd also tell herself to get an earlier start, because the more experiences a person has, the more he or she can bring to the table when tackling a large problem. "There's so much that we miss as scientists!" she laments. "We're trying to understand human behavior, but when it comes to understanding why people behave the way they do, all of us are limited to some

degree by the things we've seen and experienced. We need lots of diverse perspectives to see the big picture, so we need to get involved with community groups that can help us, like I did by becoming an EMT." Durgana believes slavery can be understood only when we understand how humans interact and behave, so the more interactions anti-traffickers can have with different kinds of people, the better.

Finally, Durgana would tell herself not to climb inside anyone else's box: "People try to push you to be a 'math person' or a 'language person,' but you can be multiple things!"

[NOTE TO YOU

Durgana desperately wants you to know that scientists can be powerful advocates for social justice. "People think of human rights as requiring a 'soft skills' set and that science is just 'hard skills,'" she says. "But if you are interested in human rights, being a scientist can help you work in this field."

She also urges you to use your gifts for the greater good. "Use your talents for languages and numbers and whatever else to help at-risk and helpless people," she says. "You can pull all your interests together to have an impact on the world. People think STEM is only about lab coat jobs, but STEM isn't limited to that. We lose people who have these passions because they don't realize that their ability with numbers can help."

[WORDS TO LIVE BY

Durgana believes anything is possible, but her other advice is this: "Always assume you can handle more than you think you can."

"I see so many promising young women undermined and convinced they are not capable," Durgana explains. "People used to underestimate me. They'd say, 'She's too smiley to be a serious scientist,' or 'Did she really write this?' because they assumed I couldn't be smart enough. Believe in your own abilities and own them. Don't second-guess yourself, because there are plenty of other people who will do that. Instead, be confident in your abilities!"

Finally, don't let other people decide what your "thing" is. "There's almost like a gendered approach to academic disciplines," says Durgana. "Writing and language are considered feminine, and people don't think of math as something women and girls are supposed to be good at, but I was, and many more of us are. Even though I was good at math, the first thing people talked about for me was my language skills. But don't let other people define you. You can be great at any number of things!"

TWO TYPES OF RESEARCH: QUANTITATIVE AND QUALITATIVE

RESEARCHERS RELY ON two types of studies: quantitative and qualitative. The difference between them is pretty easy: quantitative involves numbers (*quantities*, hence the name), while qualitative involves non-numerical data, such as stories (think of it as *quality* stories from the people you're researching). So why do we need two types, and how do researchers know when to use each one?

Sometimes it's really important just to get an accurate count of things. For example, if a new disease appears, the more people who get it, the bigger the problem is. And if the disease is fatal, it's even more serious. Say 60 percent of a population in a particular area has contracted a new disease, and that of those 60 percent, more than 80 percent of them die from it. That's a huge number of affected people, and numbers like that get attention. Based on the seriousness of the problem, the government for that particular country or region will probably devote lots more funding to treating and curing that disease than if a couple of people caught a new kind of cold that just made them sneeze a lot.

So numbers are great at telling us how big a phenomenon is, but while numbers can shock or amaze us, they don't always connect on a personal level. For example, if we tell you that there are seventy million stray animals in the United States, that might seem like a very high number. But if we show you pictures of adorable animals in terrible conditions with sad, pleading eyes, that will probably make more of an emotional impact. Qualitative research is much the same. It turns vast numbers into individuals.

In Durgana's work, both quantitative and qualitative research are crucial.

When Durgana is able to present a government with hard numbers about how many of their citizens are being enslaved, it's hard for them to say it's not happening. And when the world sees how big the problem is, the pressure is on to do something big to fight it. Much of the funding to fight slavery depends on research that proves how many people are enslaved.

At the same time, the stories from individuals sold into slavery make it impossible for people to ignore the problem or to think it can't happen to their friends and family. Sometimes big numbers can feel anonymous, making us think that the people affected by slavery are somehow different from us and that it's their problem "over there," not ours right here. But when someone tells us their story and we see ourselves and our loved ones in that individual, we want to help them.

In short, numbers appeal to our heads, but stories appeal to our hearts. And it will take both heads and hearts to bring about solutions.

EVELYN GALBAN

Providing Top Medical Care for All Creatures

[**FACT FILE**

HOMETOWN: Rochester, NY

EDUCATION: BS in Biology, Cornell University (1998); MS in Wildlife, Fish, and Wildlands, Cornell University (2002); DVM, Cornell University (2006)

EMPLOYMENT: Associate Professor of Clinical Neurology and Neurosurgery, University of Pennsylvania School of Veterinary Medicine

TOP HONORS AND ACHIEVEMENTS: Malcolm E. Miller Award for Perseverance and Scholastic Diligence (2006); Nominee for Petplan's Veterinarian of the Year (2016); Founder, Native American Veterinary Association

Chances are you know or have met a veterinarian. Maybe you also know or have met a neurosurgeon—a doctor who operates on the nervous system, including the spinal cord and the brain. But have you ever met a veterinary neurosurgeon? No? Well, allow us to introduce you to Dr. Evelyn Galban!

Galban works and teaches at the University of Pennsylvania School of Veterinary Medicine, where she is building a niche she likes to call "Zoo Neuro." This super-specialized field combines her passion for wildlife and zoo animals with her passion for neurology. You might think it's hard to work with zoo veterinarians around the world to help them with animals' neurologic problems, but hey, it's not like it's brain surgery. Oh, wait . . . yeah, it is!

While of course they're not identical to humans', animals have a nervous system, too. But the amount of attention and money devoted to understanding neurological problems in animals is significantly less than that devoted to human beings. For example, an MRI (magnetic resonance imaging) test is usually the first test run on a person when a neurological problem is suspected. But let's say your dog has symptoms of a neurological disorder. Just to get the MRI test and find out what's going on, you're looking at about $2,500. Most people simply don't have the resources to spend that kind of money on a pet. For that reason, neurological care for pets is somewhat rare (although some animal lovers can and will take any steps possible to provide the best health care available for their pets). But if a red panda or a snow leopard needed an MRI, the investment to save a member of an endangered species might seem entirely worthwhile. (For Galban, it doesn't matter whether the animal is one in a million or one *of* a million—she cares for them all!)

Zoo Neuro is such a new and specialized concept that you might wonder how Galban found herself where she is today. We wondered, too! As it turns out, Galban's life experiences actually make her the perfect fit for her field.

[THE SPARK

Evelyn grew up in both Rochester, New York, and Reno, Nevada. When she was a young child, her father went to college to pursue

a degree in electrical engineering. "I got the benefit of watching him succeed and the benefit of watching him struggle to get that degree," Galban says. (In fact, watching her mom and dad struggle in school made a big impact on Evelyn's life—but we'll explain that in a minute.) Her dad would often take her to classes with him when her mom was working and her older brother was in school, which meant that young Evelyn was exposed early to a university setting. Evelyn's mom, meanwhile, attended school intermittently and obtained a master's degree in public administration. "I watched her struggle with math and sciences," Galban recalls, "and it was amazing when she finally graduated. She was so frustrated, for example, when she had to take statistics. She did a lot of her schoolwork at home at night, and I remember once when her work was lost on the computer, and she was so upset. But eventually she was able to pass that class, even though she wasn't comfortable with STEM subjects."

Another role model was her grandmother on her mom's side. "My dad's parents both died before he was sixteen, so I never knew them," Galban explains. "But on my mother's side, both my grandparents were still living when I was a child. My grandma had a particularly strong personality. She wasn't an engineer but was heavily involved in unionization with the Institute of Electrical and Electronics Engineers because she worked on electric circuits in factories. She was extremely influential in developing that union and was a great female role model. She worked and took care of her family, and whenever I talked with her about my interest in science, she was very encouraging."

Not to say that Evelyn always wanted to become a scientist. "Very early on, I had the classic desire to be a ballerina or a pianist," she recalls. But when she was about nine or ten years old, she started going to nature camps in the summer. "I really enjoyed it," she says. "It was quite a learning experience but also fun. I remember that one of the people at the nature center offered to let us watch her do a bird autopsy. Most of the kids were grossed out, but I was more interested than disgusted! I thought it sounded neat! At that point, I knew kind of broadly that I really liked science and that I had a knack for it, so I started looking for other programs that would give me more exposure to scientific fields. By eighth grade, I got to go to a technology program at Rochester Institute of Technology, and that was amazing."

Galban says that, growing up, she was "on the nerdier side, for sure." While she played soccer throughout high school, she says, "I wasn't very good at it. But it was an outlet for my energy because I really liked to run. And I got to experience the feeling of being part of a team." She most enjoyed just reading and being out in nature. Socially, she "tried really hard to be easy to get along with and kind of mix in between different groups in school."

Her main focus, though, was academic success. "I was determined to be really good in school," she says. "My parents supported me but didn't put pressure on me. They didn't have to. The pressure was self-imposed. In fact, my mom would sometimes force me to take what she called 'me days' off from school because she worried that I was driving myself too hard." Evelyn's public high school was highly academically competitive, and although she was a serious student, she wasn't the class valedictorian. "I guess I was probably in the top twenty in terms of GPA, but I wasn't the smartest person in the class," she says. "But I had some great teachers who were strong mentors and role models."

One of her most adored teachers wasn't in math or science, but in French. "I took French throughout high school," Galban says, "and Mr. Thomas was someone I really admired. We had a great connection as student and teacher. I felt comfortable asking him for advice about how to best study in school or where to apply to college." Additionally, her AP Biology teacher, Ms. Bailey, did Evelyn a solid by giving her special permission to take the course early. "Usually, AP Bio was a class for seniors only, but Ms. Bailey let me take it as a sophomore so that I could take more sciences in high school. And it was such a wonderful class. The way she introduced topics, you could tell she really looked through the material and found the stuff that would most trigger our imaginations and grab our attention."

During those early years of high school, Evelyn's mom started trying to help her choose a college to attend. "We traveled to Cornell, about an hour and a half away from home," says Galban. "I fell in love instantly with the beautiful campus. It's

a large campus, but being surrounded by the laid-back town of Ithaca gives it a smaller feel. I knew instantly that Cornell was the only place I wanted to go. I knew also that I wanted to study science there, but there were so many options in science that I decided to just go for a general biology degree. Our family wasn't extremely wealthy, so we didn't know if we could make it financially if I went to a private university. But they have a state school portion that allowed me to go while paying in-state tuition."

During college, Evelyn gravitated toward medical sciences and thought she would go on to study medicine. "But then I realized that would mean working with sick people who might get sick *on* me," she says. "One of my internships was at the National

Institute on Aging, where we worked with rabbits, and I realized that I didn't mind caring for the rabbits if they were sick. I wasn't grossed out by sick animals, just sick people!" That's when she began thinking about a career as a veterinarian.

Working with animals felt like a natural fit for Evelyn. She attributes her early respect for animals to her Washoe and Paiute heritage. "We believe that every living thing is worthy of respect and love," Galban explains. "I see my animal patients as family and friends to their people, and doctors should always do the best we can for our patients and their families. My dad is a member of the Washoe Tribe of Nevada and California, and I grew up as part of a multitribal group called American Indians of All Nations. One of the key principles we shared is that everything is related, that the health of one of us means the health of all of us, and that we all deserve the same amount of respect. In that sense, treating a dog patient is no different than treating a human patient." Veterinary school, therefore, seemed like the perfect fit.

Problem was, Evelyn was already in her senior year of college and had not been preparing to apply for a slot in veterinary school. As a result, she didn't get in on her first try . . . or her second. "When I first applied to vet school, I was missing an academic requirement on the application, and I was missing experience," she explains. (Most applicants to veterinary schools have done internships and taken classes related to animals, making their applications more impressive in this highly competitive admissions field.) The second time she applied, she was still missing a required undergraduate physics course. "I had actually taken the class but hadn't done well because there was no instructor. You were just supposed to read a book and take tests. That wasn't my learning style."

At this point, a lot of people might have just given up, but not

Evelyn. She took the physics class again and reapplied to veterinary school. "I definitely had a plan B lined up," she recalls. "Of course, I was thinking, 'What if I never get accepted?'" So while she waited, she got a master's degree in wildlife science. "I figured it would do a couple of things: one, improve my application to vet school, and two, give me another skill set. I was determined. I remember telling my dad that even if I had to go get a PhD first, I would eventually get into vet school! Not being accepted the first couple of times was crushing at first, but then I realized I had to just take a step back and see what I could do to make it happen. I reached out for help to the people in admissions about how I could improve my chances of getting in. It was embarrassing to ask for help, but now that I'm on the other side of the admissions process, as a professor training students, I realize I had no reason to feel embarrassed. We want to offer help. That's why we're here."

On her third try, Evelyn got in to veterinary school. This is the part of the story where everything should be smooth sailing toward Galban's happy ending, isn't it?

But that's not how it went.

"My next failure was much larger than not getting into vet school twice," Galban says. "I also failed my board exams twice." Board exams are the big standardized licensing tests physicians and veterinarians have to take after they complete their coursework and years of training. If they don't pass those board exams, all their hard work was for nothing: they don't get to become specialized doctors. "You'd think that after three years of residency in neurology and neurosurgery, I'd have been well prepared for the board exam," explains Galban. "But there are five parts to the exam, and four of them are short answer and essay. I did fine with those sections. But one section of the test is multiple-choice, and I struggled so hard with it. I'm not sure why multiple-choice is difficult for me, but it is. So I failed the first time by a few multiple-choice questions. Then when I took the board exam again, I failed by one question." Talk about heartbreaking!

"I had some serious self-doubt when I failed the board exam those two times," she says. "But I knew I couldn't focus on that. I had to push those self-defeating thoughts out of my head and focus on the task at hand. I had to buckle down, try again, and really calm myself down, because managing the stress of the exam was about nine-tenths of the problem."

Remember all those years before when young Evelyn watched her dad struggle to get his degree in electrical engineering and her mom struggle with her statistics class? Evelyn certainly remembered. She reached out to her parents and drew from their experiences. "Electrical engineers have to take a class in thermodynamics in order to graduate," says Galban. "My dad struggled so hard with that course. He had to take it three times. So when I started to think I couldn't pass my boards, I thought of Dad sitting at the kitchen table with his head in his hands. Of course he doubted himself, but I remembered how, after failing the class twice, he got up from that table and said, 'Next time, I'm going to do it. I'm going to get there.' I thought of my mom losing all her hard work for that statistics class on the computer that night so many years before, and how she had to redo all of it. And I realized that after you process the initial disappointment, it's all about making a plan. You have to break it down and say, 'OK, this is what I'm going to do every day to get where I need to be.' Set those tiny goals for each and every day."

Obviously, it worked, because now you're reading about Dr. Galban in this book! And her parents are so proud of her and so happy that their positive responses to adversity made such an impact on their daughter that they'd take thermodynamics and statistics a dozen more times if they had to. (But they're very glad they don't have to!)

[THE EUREKA MOMENT

Galban's first eureka moment came when she homed in on her specialty. She found herself fascinated by specific cases that occasionally surfaced at area zoos. "After an exciting consult with a cheetah who had developed a seizure disorder, I thought about ways I could build the caseload," Galban explains. "There is no neurologist currently filling this niche. Most see a case here and there. I want to become the neurologist that people think of when they need a zoo-oriented neuro nerd! Before I followed the winding road to where I am now, I had planned to become a zoo specialist, but I'd changed my mind at the last minute when I chose my residency program. Now I want to return to that other passion and develop myself in that direction, follow that flow."

Other eureka moments come on a case-by-case basis. For example, Galban recalls one particular story of an Irish setter. She can't share his name for reasons of patient confidentiality, but we'll call him Lucky (because, as you'll see, he was one lucky dog to have Galban as his veterinarian!). Lucky's human brought him to see Galban when Lucky was six months old and had suddenly lost his balance. At the time, Galban was still a resident (a vet in training). Galban ordered an MRI of Lucky's brain and then performed a spinal tap (taking fluid from the spinal column in order to study it). The MRI showed changes characteristic of meningitis (inflammation of the covering of the brain), and the fluid from the spinal tap contained a fungus.

"It took my going to meet with the infectious-disease people at the human hospital to develop a protocol, because what [Lucky] had was cryptococcal meningitis, a disease of dogs that's very uncommon and difficult for them to survive. I put him on the suggested protocol with a drug that was newer at the time. He was on that for about a year and did OK with it until he relapsed. We had to find new options for him, all of which were potentially life-threatening. We got rid of most of the fungus in his system, but then he had a change in his neurologic signs, which told me that something else had happened."

Galban ordered another MRI, this time of Lucky's spinal cord, and learned that he'd developed a pocket of fluid from his original illness. They tested the fluid and found that the original fungus was back. Galban performed surgery, and Lucky lived much longer than he would have without her care.

The lesson here? In actual patient care, it often takes a determined physician like Galban who's willing to stay on the case until the best answer can be found.

[NOTE TO SELF

If Galban could go back and talk to her younger self, she'd give her some advice she picked up in veterinary school. "When I was graduating, one of our instructors said something incredible, and that was 'You need to be uncomfortable.' That's so true. So I'd tell my childhood and teen self that she needs to leave her comfort zone so that she'll be able to grow. That was very hard for me to learn early on. Being nervous and embracing change was a big struggle for me, so I'd tell myself to just embrace change and new environments."

[NOTE TO YOU

Galban realizes that some of you already know exactly what you want to do, while others . . . not so much. "Some may just know that STEM is interesting to them, and that's not a bad thing," she says. "It's great to keep it broad in the early stages and reach out to programs that interest you and search for things." For her, the American Indian Science and Engineering Society helped her see what was available. "They have a large focus on students in high school and college," she explains. "They have a national meeting and a quarterly magazine, and having exposure to that let me see all the things available out there. I learned where I could go, what I could learn, and I found people like me who could serve as role models. Find an organization like that for you!"

[WORDS TO LIVE BY

"I don't know if this is my top life advice, but if it's not, it's a close runner-up," says Galban. "And it's something my dad would say to me when I was younger: 'Stay in balance.' He would say it when he thought I was working too hard, or when he thought maybe I was watching too much TV. You can have too much work or too much play. You need some of both."

Another concept Galban likes? Flow. "I think 'flow' may be kind of a buzzword now," she says. "But every day, we're faced with challenges, and you can bring everything back to flow, which is this idea that there's an optimum experience that pushes you to your limits, and in that sweet spot, that's where you grow. If I could achieve that flow, I'd be perfect! So I when I speak to high school kids, I always tell them to find their flow."

THE FUTURE OF MEDICINE? CLICK "PRINT"

YOU'VE PROBABLY HEARD about 3-D printers, which are so amazing in general that it's hard to believe they even exist! But beyond just being cool, 3-D printing has incredible implications for the future of medicine. Researchers have so far been able to 3-D print a robot hand that plays the piano, a prototype for a bionic eye, and implants that can help regrow injured nerves. For neurologists like Galban, this could eventually mean better chances for repairing injured spinal cords.

Another helpful aspect of 3-D printing, particularly for neurology, is that it is now possible to 3-D print a replica of the brain. Just imagine the pressure involved for brain surgeons during their first surgery! 3-D printing of the brain allows them to have some practice before working on the real thing. Sure, medical schools use brains from cadavers (dead bodies) and animals for practice, but not all brains are alike. And even for nonsurgical interventions, it's helpful to have a model to work from. For example, it would be difficult for a doctor-in-training to study schizophrenia using an animal's brain because only humans suffer from this particular disease.

3-D printing in medicine goes beyond just implants, robotics, and models, though. As you may know, organ donation saves many lives, but there aren't enough donors for all the patients who need new organs. Many patients are put on waiting lists, and some may die before they ever get the organ they need. Even when an organ is available, there's always a risk that the patient who receives a donated organ may "reject" it—that his or her body may recognize the new organ not as a helper, but instead as a dangerous intruder. When that happens, the patient's immune system will fight the new organ, and this can result in a failed procedure or even death. A version of 3-D printing called bioprinting uses a patient's own stem cells to print tissue from their nervous system. Bioprinting is still in the early stages, but the hope is that someday it could eliminate the need for an outside donor because doctors could use the patient's own stem cells to 3-D print the tissue needed to create a new organ. Incredible!

CIERRA McDONALD

Using Computer Science for Serious Fun

[FACT FILE

HOMETOWN: Chicago, IL

EDUCATION: BS in Computer Science (Engineering), University of Illinois at Urbana-Champaign (2003); Certificate in Game Design, University of Washington (2012)

EMPLOYMENT: Principal Program Manager for Xbox, Microsoft

TOP HONORS AND ACHIEVEMENTS: Inaugural Recipient of the Industry Image Award, International Game Developers Association Blacks in Games Special Interest Group (2017); Jerry A. Lawson Award for Achievement in Game Development, IGDA Foundation (2019); Speaker for Girls Who Code, DigiGirlz, and GeekGirlCon

Just about everyone has some interest in computer games, whether it's your friend who has dominated every secret level of a particular blockbuster phenomenon or your granddad who just plays solitaire on his phone. While most video games aren't designed to save the world or cure a terrible disease (although scientists have actually used gamers to help with disease research—check out *Foldit* as one example), they do provide something important: fun! For many people, video games provide a chance to unwind, reduce stress, and form communities. (They can also be a great educational tool!) Gaming has come a long way from its humble beginnings—seriously, ask your parents or grandparents to describe a 1970s game called *Pong*. When they tell you it was two lines batting a dot back and forth on a television screen, you'll think they're kidding, but back in the day, this was state-of-the-art technology.

Compare *Pong* to the popular video games of today that, with their breathtaking art and fluid animation, allow us to practically become a character in a movie, and you can appreciate how far computer gaming technology has come. But these leaps in technology didn't just happen. Gaming companies employ large teams of extremely talented people.

One of those people is Cierra McDonald, principal program manager at Xbox. McDonald's job description is so broad that it's hard to list all the things she does, but her primary job is to make sure the Xbox systems fit customer needs and that game developers get all the help they need in creating new games. McDonald, a computer science engineer, allows developers to focus on the creative side while she and her team make sure the games work flawlessly. (Turn to page 49 to find out just how involved the process truly is.) To that end, McDonald has helped invent several features for Xbox, including a way to archive gamer achievements.

Achievements are bonuses that developers embed in individual games to provide virtual high fives to gamers who demonstrate exceptional prowess. Achievements offer players a chance to take on extra challenges on top of tackling the game's overall objective. A gamer has to do something extra cool to unlock a certain achievement, and when that unlocking happens, it's usually accompanied by a happy sound and a pop-up announcing the achievement. Achievements come with extra points that add to your Gamerscore (Xbox's measure of gaming awesomeness), but they're also just nice little pats on the back.

One thing that concerned McDonald about achievements was that sometimes gamers could miss these well-deserved accolades. For example, if a gamer did something achievement-worthy at the exact moment her Wi-Fi cut out unexpectedly, that would be a real drag. McDonald, not wanting gamers to miss a single moment of glory, made sure that Xbox began keeping a record of gamers' achievements so that these successes could be relived. Because, hey, if your character survives all manner of peril and saves the day, you deserve your moment!

Thinking about every aspect of gaming and how to make it even more rewarding and interactive is what McDonald does every single day. What's especially interesting is that, while she's now helping gamers connect to one another worldwide, she started out as an only child playing games all by herself.

[THE SPARK

For most of her childhood, Cierra was the only child of a single mom on the South Side of Chicago. (She has a little sister, but she wasn't born until Cierra was almost fifteen.) Cierra's mother was a certified public accountant (CPA) who handled corporate audits for the Internal Revenue Service. In addition to working with numbers, CPAs have to know tons of intricate tax laws, so in some ways, they're kind of like lawyers with calculators. That meant that Cierra's mom was good at both mathematics and language skills. Additionally, she had an outstanding work ethic. "She pushed herself, and she pushed me," says McDonald. "She held a high bar but also believed that I could meet it. She would recognize and acknowledge my accomplishments but also push me when she knew I could do better. Really, she didn't have to push much because I always knew what she expected, and I thought I could deliver, so it was more of an internal drive to challenge myself."

Cierra's mom got her into the city's best magnet schools and enrolled her in after-school programs to keep her mind busy, but McDonald notes that her mom never forced her into activities she didn't like, instead focusing on Cierra's actual interests. "I loved logic puzzles," McDonald recalls. "I didn't realize they were math things; I just loved them. So my mom found a program where we did lots of logic exercises. She always really challenged me, and I think that's why I still challenge myself." McDonald also notes that her mother was an avid reader, something she picked up from her early on. Reading provided a fun way for Cierra, as an only child, to occupy herself when her mom was at work or brought work home with her. Another pastime Cierra enjoyed? Playing board games. Alone.

"I played a lot of multiplayer board games by myself," she says. "I'd be three different players, but at the beginning of each game, I decided which player was actually me, and I'd keep score. I always stuck to whatever 'my' score was, even if I was losing. I'd play pick-up sticks this way as well as board games such as Sorry! The name of that particular game makes it sound really sad, but I enjoyed myself!"

Cierra's mom had a personal computer at a time when computers weren't so prevalent in American homes. When Cierra was about twelve years old, she checked out a book on computer programming. "It was out of sheer boredom," McDonald recalls.

"Back then, computers weren't everywhere, and there were no cell phones, so there weren't as many things available to distract kids. We had to find stuff to do. So I got this book, and it was about BASIC, a computer language. I was reading it and kind of understanding it, and kind of not understanding it, but they had code examples. The book said you could have a conversation with a computer, that it could talk to you. So on the not-very-fancy computer we had, there was a program I could run in BASIC and execute it so that the computer would say, 'What is your name?' and you'd enter it and it would say, 'Hello, Cierra.' Then it would ask about your favorite color and things like that. So that was kind of my *aha!* moment about computer science. Before that, I had used computers only to write a paper or play an occasional game. I had learned DOS [disk operating system, computer software that allows a computer to perform basic functions] by installing games on floppy disks, because my mom didn't know how to do that and was like, 'You figure it out.' But this coding book taught me that I could do other stuff with a computer and that there were people behind it. Somebody had to make it work. So I changed some lines out of the book, and that, to me, felt really dangerous because we didn't have much money, and I was worried that I would break something if I experimented with the computer. I knew that if I broke it, we couldn't necessarily replace it. But I saw that, oh, wow, I could change some things without breaking it! That was how I learned what programming was."

It was Cierra's uncle Derrick, who was fifteen years older than she, who first introduced her to a video game console. "Derrick was not a huge gamer himself, but he is the same sort of engineering nerd I am, so he always liked gadgets and tech. He bought an original Nintendo when I was about three years old. He was more like a brother to me, and he gave me that Nintendo."

Derrick went on to study computer science at the University of Illinois at Urbana-Champaign, eventually getting a PhD in the subject. "Derrick wasn't around much because he was so much older that he was either in school or working," McDonald recalls. "But when he visited, we would 'talk shop.' He'd tell me about his computers, and we'd talk about gadgets and stuff. He was the person I would talk to about what I wanted to be when I grew up. Of course, at that time, I wanted to be a scientist in a lab. I was so little that I didn't really understand what that meant. I thought scientists made everything, from food to furniture, *poof!*, in a lab! But later on when I came to understand what computer science was, thanks in large part to Derrick, that began to appeal to me."

Another great support system for Cierra was her grand-parents. Her grandfather, an Air Force veteran, instilled in his children and grandchildren a strong work ethic, thriftiness, and respect for others. Though neither of her grandparents had college degrees themselves, it was important to them that their children and grandchildren obtain them. "They are very proud that all of their seven children have college degrees," McDonald says.

While Cierra was toward the top of her class in school, she says, "I thought of myself as a 'geek' only in a positive sense because I thought of doing well in school as a good thing. Really, I thought of myself as sort of floating between these different cliques and identities, because in addition to taking these AP and honors courses, I was also a bit of a class clown and would crack jokes and try to be funny. On my old report cards, it's kind of crazy how many notes teachers wrote about how I was smart but needed to focus on school instead of talking to other students! One reason my mom may have had me in all those after-school activities was because I needed help burning off some intellectual energy!"

That still left plenty of energy for sports, though. Cierra played basketball and ran track, and she loved a good game of kickball. Often, she would be one of the few girls—or the only girl—interested in such things. "In some ways, it made me feel a little disconnected to other girls. I preferred a pickup basketball game with the boys during recess. And then, as I got more into math and science, it was mostly boys in my classes who were good at that stuff, so most of my friends were either boys or girls from my basketball team. Outside of school, I wasn't part of the popular crew that people were trying to hang out with. I was gregarious but more naturally introverted—I just wasn't emotionally driven to seek out time with other people so much. I felt at times that people liked me only when I said something interesting or funny or was useful to them in some other way, but outside of school, they weren't inviting me to do things. Sometimes I didn't feel like I had real friends, at least not until I got into high school."

Additionally, no teachers took a particular interest in her. "My teachers were fine, but I can't say I remember by name any one of them as being particularly influential," McDonald says. "I went to multiple schools throughout my childhood, so that's one reason it's hard to remember specific teachers. However, I went to a preschool called Villa Pre, deep on the South Side of Chicago, and they taught me how to read by the time I was four—and not just basic reading but pretty decently advanced. People have a perception of the South Side of Chicago as being a wasteland or a war zone, but they forget the human side of it, which is that there are people there who live and work and love their families. My preschool was great. Even though I never had any interest in becoming, say, an English major, I have always performed well on verbal and reading sections of standardized tests, only slightly lower than my math scores, and I give a lot of the credit to that early childhood education."

Those standardized test scores did not go unnoticed as Cierra progressed in high school. Several universities tried to recruit her. "I started getting unsolicited pamphlets in the mail, I guess because of my test scores," she recalls. Cierra began researching different colleges. By this point, she knew she wanted to major in computer science, so she came up with a list of her top six or seven school choices, none of which were the University of Illinois at Urbana-Champaign, where she ultimately wound up.

"Illinois had a strong computer science program," McDonald says, "but I wanted to go a little farther away and be on my own. But that thriftiness and practicality my grandparents had always taught us made the difference. By the time I got to junior year in high school and looked at our finances realistically, I figured Illinois made a lot of sense! And it really is a great school—people come from out of state to go there. My grandparents had retired in a town about thirty minutes from campus, so from a pragmatic standpoint, it just made sense." And, of course, it was her uncle Derrick's alma mater.

"My uncle introduced me to a dean named Paul Parker, who'd been a dean there when Derrick was an undergraduate student also. Dean Parker became my first mentor before I knew what a mentor even was. He told me about NSBE, National Society of Black Engineers. I joined that group, and all of us spent a lot of time together and really bonded. It was like a family. It's so important to find an anchor like that in the fast-paced environment of college life, where it's easy to struggle. I think NSBE and Dean Parker were both a huge part of my success in college."

[THE EUREKA MOMENT

Because McDonald works on a large team at Xbox, she doesn't feel comfortable claiming personal responsibility for their big innovations. "What we do is large and complex enough that it would be hard to point to one person who is responsible for everything," she explains. "Even though I have some patents for things I have worked on or driven, I didn't do that work in isolation, even when I may have spearheaded things."

However, McDonald designed and was responsible for the backend system that enables the achievement systems used in Xbox 360, Xbox One, Windows iOS, and Windows phones. Achievements, as explained earlier, are rewards within games for players who perfectly complete difficult tasks. They don't have value outside the game (you can't cash them in for prizes or anything like that), but most gamers agree that achievements are nothing short of awesome because they're fun and they increase your overall Gamerscore. "I added a bunch of features on top of achievements," McDonald says. Some of those include allowing players to see how close they are to unlocking an achievement, and giving them a big, sparkly diamond for unlocking rare achievements. The concept of "achievement rarity" is one that McDonald had a hand in—basically, some achievements are unlocked by only a tiny percentage of gamers, and those achievements get special recognition, undoubtedly a proud moment for the valiant few!

But being so tied in with making gaming even more fun has its downside. McDonald—whose own Gamerscore is over 100,000—notes a common response when people find out what she does for a living. "They often ask me if I can boost their score for them." Sorry, but no, she can't!

You might think that being in such a creative field means that

McDonald's bright ideas come to her in flashes of inspiration. But while some big ideas are born of serendipity, others come from day-in, day-out planning and strategizing. McDonald insists that her big ideas don't just pop into her brain unexpectedly. "I like to think, so I'm much less random with ideas," she explains. "The ideas I generate are generally the product of intentionally thinking about my work."

[NOTE TO SELF

Looking back on her childhood and teen years, McDonald would give her former self one important message: "There is no one way to be a girl."

"What I mean by that," she explains, "is that while girls feel a lot of pressure from society and from themselves to fit into a mold, whoever you are, whatever you are, whatever you like or are good at, that *is* what girls like or are good at! It's not, 'Oh, you must like these things, and if you don't, you should feel embarrassed.' Maybe others won't share your interests and maybe some people will make you try to conform, but be confident in what you like because it's OK to be you. Doing 'geeky' things and being interested in STEM or whatever doesn't have to be popular with anyone else. You are welcome to have your own interests. And if those interests are so unique that other people don't get it, then guess what? You may be blazing a new trail so that other people can like it, too."

[NOTE TO YOU

McDonald has one word for you: "DABBLE."

She explains, "Now more than ever, there's so much access to information and tools, and so much of it is free, so play around with stuff! You don't have to be afraid to break things. I mean, don't be cavalier with your parents' money, but get out there and try something. If you don't like it, that's fine, too. But the earlier you start, the sooner you'll know what you like and don't like. Learning as you go is a great thing, and when you're young and don't have so many responsibilities piled on you is the time to try stuff."

She'd also like you to know that you don't have to be a computer scientist or an engineer to become part of the video gaming industry. "People who work for gaming companies don't have to be STEM majors," she says. "We need music people and artists and lawyers as well as engineers. So don't put a lid on yourself. Don't think there's no career path related to your interests, whatever they are. Don't think you have to do what other people want you to do. Investigate now what's right for you."

[WORDS TO LIVE BY

McDonald's words of wisdom? "Eat your vegetables first!" But she's not necessarily talking about your eating habits.

"I often say this to myself, to my mentees, and to my team," she explains. "It comes from when I was a kid. At dinnertime, I would eat all of the veggies like cabbage or green beans off my plate first, and then I would slowly savor the good stuff that remained—the stuff I actually enjoyed eating, like mashed potatoes, creamed corn, garlic bread, and macaroni and cheese.

"Basically, it means get the hard stuff out of the way up front. If there's a task or project that seems difficult—or unclear, or confusing, or simply unfun—drive straight into it and handle it right away. Don't put it off and dillydally on the stuff that's easy, or quick, or fun.

"If I follow this strategy, I can get the necessary yet unpleasant work done with as much time remaining as possible, and then I can turn my full attention to enjoying the quick or fun work and have full confidence that I won't get caught off guard by that pesky unpleasant work I might have otherwise put off. After all, who wants to eat all of the good stuff and then just have a plate full of vegetables staring back at them?"

For the record, McDonald actually loves vegetables now! But, she says, "The spirit of the thing still applies!"

IT TAKES A VILLAGE: HOW VIDEO GAMES ARE MADE

LOVE VIDEO GAMES? You could get a job making them! You don't even have to be a straight-up STEM person: the video game industry employs people with a wide variety of backgrounds, including musicians, artists, and actors.

The creation of a video game is not a linear process. That is to say, it doesn't go from one step to the next like an assembly line. Instead, many people work together simultaneously until the product is complete. Naturally, the bigger the video game's budget, the more people who are involved, but here's a basic idea of how the process works. . . .

Concept: Like anything else, video games begin with an idea. Ideas can come from anywhere, but game designers are often inspired by other games, much the same way filmmakers are inspired by one another's movies. *Game designers* develop the vision for a game and how it will work, and they may either write a game's script themselves or employ *writers* to assist them. Once the concept is ready, it's passed along to a *producer*, who manages the team and keeps the project on track to be completed on time. While handling all of that, the producer also oversees the next steps: art, sound, and programming, all of which are happening in a loop as the team members work together.

Art: The first step in art is to create a storyboard along with the writers. This is basically just a scene-by-scene rough draft of the game; at this stage, characters aren't fully fleshed out, and scenery isn't detailed. An *art director* coordinates the look and feel of the game's art and leads a team, consisting of a *concept artist*, who decides what the characters, props, environments, and visual effects will look like; a *technical artist* or *front-end artist*, who helps translate the artist's design into code for the game; and a *3-D artist*, who creates the in-game content. Companies may have different 3-D artists who focus on characters, environments, or props. Sometimes 3-D artists work with people wearing special suits with 3-D sensors to make the characters' movements more realistic. (Animators responsible for this type of motion capture usually work with art tools instead of actual coding.) *Visual effects artists* make the explosions and special effects; *lighting artists* make sure all the game's scenes are properly lit. With such attention to characters and environments, games are so detailed that they may look like an actual movie, with scenery so realistic it appears to have been filmed.

Sound: A *sound designer* chooses music and sounds for the game. Games with bigger budgets may hire a *composer* to watch the game and score an original soundtrack for it. *Audio engineers* record and mix the sounds in a recording studio, and *voice actors* bring characters to life just like other actors do in movies and television. If necessary, a *music supervisor* obtains legal rights for sounds or music already in existence (not created by a composer specifically for the game).

Programming: There are too many software developers and computer programmers involved in video game creation to list all of the specific jobs, but a few include *gameplay engineers*, who design the game's software; *server engineers*, who put the mechanisms required for the game to work correctly onto the server; and *graphics programmers*, who solve graphics problems, "debug" games (fix glitches), and design graphics. All these and other coding experts write the computer code that makes the game work properly. Often this involves using artificial intelligence (AI) to allow gamers a myriad of choices about what can happen inside a game.

Other: "Other" is a big umbrella when it comes to video games, since after the game itself is made, much of the work is just beginning! Completed games must be tested, marketed to the public, and distributed for sale. *Quality assurance testers* play games for hours on end to check for bugs (you may be thinking, "Wow, tough life!" but it actually is hard work!). When they find bugs, they report them to developers so they can be fixed. Meanwhile, *marketing executives*, *sales representatives*, and *finance managers* are working to build hype, get the game into stores, and handle the business side of things!

*Thank you to Andrew Dennis, an instructor at Michigan State University's program for game design and development, for his help on this section. In addition to offering a top-ranked games development undergraduate program, MSU also offers one-week programs for high school students interested in the gaming industry, even if the students have no previous experience in game design. Check it out at https://comartsci.msu.edu/camps. With a little internet research, you can probably find similar programs at universities in your area.

PATRÍCIA MEDICI

Saving the Tapirs (and Rain Forests . . .
and Woods . . . and Grasslands)

[**FACT FILE**

HOMETOWN: São Caetano do Sul, São Paulo, Brazil

EDUCATION: Bachelor's Degree in Forestry Sciences, Universidade de São Paulo (1995); Master's Degree in Wildlife Ecology, Conservation, and Management, Universidade Federal de Minas Gerais (2001); PhD in Biodiversity Management, University of Kent (2010)

EMPLOYMENT: Research Coordinator, Lowland Tapir Conservation Initiative, Instituto de Pesquisas Ecológicas; Chair, International Union for Conservation of Nature's Species Survival Commission's Tapir Specialist Group

HONORS AND ACHIEVEMENTS: Future for Nature Award, Future for Nature Foundation (2008); Whitley Award, Whitley Fund for Nature (2008); TED Fellow (2014)

Perhaps you've never heard of a tapir. (Make up for it on page 63.) If you haven't, you probably also haven't heard of Dr. Patrícia Medici, who has quietly dedicated most of her adult life to saving these amazing animals in her native Brazil. Lucky for our planet that Patrícia Medici isn't in it for the publicity, because her work is extremely important. Those tapirs most people have never heard of actually play an extremely important role in balancing

the ecosystem. And studying tapirs? Well, it's no piece of cake.

Tapirs are tough animals to track down. They don't run in packs, preferring a more solitary existence. And they're nocturnal, so when they do come out, it's at night. Once Medici and her team find a tapir, they have to capture it for a short time and put it to sleep, then put a tracking device on it so they can keep up with the animal to study it. When the tapir wakes up, it has a snazzy new piece of bling around its neck that not only tracks its movements but also protects it from being hit by cars. (When Medici kept seeing dead tapirs on the side of the highway, she got the idea to put reflective tape on the collars so that motorists might see these endangered animals before they plow them down. Every tapir saved is a win in the battle against extinction!)

As a little girl, Patrícia Medici never saw herself growing up to save the tapirs. Like many of us, she'd never even heard of them. She had different plans for her future, but in what turned out to be a fortunate turn of events for the tapirs, someone changed young Patrícia's life. How? By boring her to death! No, really! Read on. . . .

[THE SPARK

Patrícia was born in Brazil to a mother who "couldn't have been more resilient," Medici says. Her mother didn't have a college education or a professional background, but she was extremely hardworking, loving, and funny. She married Patrícia's father, an Italian businessman who imported candy, when he moved to Brazil in his thirties. The couple divorced when Patrícia was just two years old, and her father moved back to Italy, so she never knew him well. Patrícia's mother then married a nice German man who'd moved to Brazil, and they had Patrícia's half brother. Unfortunately, Patrícia's stepdad died when she was eight and her brother was only ten months old, so her mother took whatever jobs she could find, selling things or working as a secretary. This meant that Patrícia became her brother's babysitter, a job she didn't mind much as it allowed her to spend time with the only sibling she knew. "My father was married in Italy twice before coming to Brazil, and he had three kids in Italy," she says. "They were much older. I've never met them, but I have communicated with them. He married someone else in Brazil before he met my mom, and they had two kids together. When I was a teenager, my mom used to joke that whenever I started dating someone, I'd better bring him to the house so we could make sure he wasn't my brother! She had such a great sense of humor."

Although Patrícia had only a short time with her stepfather before he died, a decision he and her mother made together wound up having a big impact on Patrícia's future. "When my mom married my stepdad, we moved to the middle of the Atlantic Forest," she explains. "It was amazing! All kinds of animals, even monkeys, all over the place! There were so many trails to explore because we had one of the very first houses in the area. We were right next to a big lake. It was so beautiful.

Suddenly, here I was, exposed to nature and animals. I loved walking in the forest and playing and building huts and stuff."

But her stepfather's death brought many challenges. Medici says, "We had a really tough life. My poor mom was divorced and now widowed with a baby and an eight-year-old. She couldn't get really good jobs because she didn't have a college education or professional training. I had to become very independent because I had to help her. That's why I started working early in my life. I would take jobs babysitting or whatever when I was a teenager. When I went to college, my mom had to sell a bunch of stuff for me to be able to afford to go, and I had to get a job as soon as I started."

Although she was always at the top of her class, Medici emphasizes that she had to work hard to get there. "I was always very responsible," she says. "I had to develop that sense of independence and responsibility at a young age in order to succeed in life. My scores were always perfect, so I was part nerd, but I was never one of those kids who didn't have to study, who could get the good score without working."

In spite of her hard work, Patrícia maintained a sense of humor. "I always loved to be funny and was usually the life of the party," she says. "I was a weird combination, I guess. I never felt that I didn't fit in, even though I wasn't able to play sports or do many things like that since we didn't have a lot of money. There was a swimming pool near our house, but we couldn't afford lessons, so my mom told me, 'Teach yourself how to swim and don't die.' So I taught myself to swim. I'd explore the trails, and I'd kayak across the lake and back."

Patrícia attended the same primary school for her first eight years of her education and had many of the same teachers more than once, some of whom she stays in touch with to this day. "It was a really healthy childhood for me, living in that wonderful house in the forest," Medici says. "I would walk to school, come back, shower, eat my food in a few bites, and then do my homework so I could get outside as soon as possible." Plenty of friends were always ready to join in the fun, too. "Friends liked to come to my house to play outside," she recalls. "My mom's policy was that when you are a teenager and you want to hang out somewhere, you'll do it here. She said, 'This house is a place you can bring your friends.' And of course everyone loved coming to my house because there was so much to do and everybody also loved my mom."

Although her family and friends loved the house in the forest, Patrícia's mother eventually had to make the painful decision to move. "My teachers in primary school kept telling my mom, 'You have to get her out of here.' They urged her to move so I that I could go to high school somewhere else because the teaching at the high school wasn't good where I was. It's different the way it works in Brazil: there's no such thing as a scholarship to college because the public universities are free, *if* you can pass the test to get in. But to pass those tests, you have to be extremely well prepared, and the only way to be prepared is to go to a private high school because that's the best system. But of course, you have to pay for private high school. So wealthy people get to go to the good high schools, and they are the ones who get into public universities. It is really unfair. Families like mine without money for private high school can never hope to get their children into the public universities. So after ten years at our home in the forest, my mom moved us to São Paulo City. Then she went knocking on the doors of the best schools—private schools we could not pay for—asking for scholarships. That's how I went to one of the best schools in São Paulo, and that's how I got into college."

Right before graduating high school, Patrícia changed her mind about what she wanted to study in college. "When I was little, I wanted to be different things: a veterinarian, an astronaut, an archeologist," she says. "But as I got a little older, I decided I wanted to be an architect. I have zero idea where that came from, but I think I decided to be an architect because they make good money, and I wanted to help my mom financially, so I thought I should do that." Getting into college is stressful for any student, but if you're dreading the ACT or SAT, consider yourself lucky: in Brazil, there's no such thing as a standardized college entrance exam that is universally accepted. Each university has its own killer exam students have to take to see if they can get in. Since each university has its very own exam, it was as though Patrícia had to take the SAT over and over again. "It was super tough," she recalls. "I absolutely had to get into a public university because we couldn't afford a private one. So I was studying day and night, thinking I was going to become an architect." Her plans changed, though, thanks to a career fair at her school.

"My school had this weekend towards the end of the year where all these professionals would come—doctors, lawyers, teachers, architects, engineers, and so forth—and you could talk to them. A friend and I went together and talked to this architect, and he couldn't have been more boring," Medici says. "I had all these questions about designs and what his life was like, and he was just super boring, and I thought, 'I don't want to be an architect! Look at this guy!'

"Luckily, my friend wanted to be a forestry engineer, and though I had no idea what that was, I went with her to talk to a professional in that area. This guy was super interesting and excited about his work. He talked about wildlife management, and I told him I was kind of interested in animals, and as he talked with me about that, his eyes were just shining with enthusiasm. So I went back later to hear a speech he'd prepared, and I was so impressed with how he talked about how great it was to be a forestry engineer, so I took the exams to become one. It was a pretty sudden move. I remember my mom said, 'Well, this doesn't sound all that responsible. Yesterday you wanted to be an architect and today you want to be a . . . what?' But she said it was OK with her. Unfortunately, this particular course of study was available only at a university outside of our town, so to pursue it, I had to move away from home, which meant I had to pay for housing and make all sorts of other financial arrangements while I was there. It cost more to study this, but by then, I was confident that it was what I wanted to do."

[THE EUREKA MOMENT

Not all scientific successes have a cool anecdote behind them. "I always make jokes that I don't have a very romantic story," Medici says. "Lots of conservationists have been in love with the species they work with since they were little, but that's not the way it was with me. I had no idea what tapirs were when I was growing up. When I went to college, I was doing an internship at a breeding center at my university. They had a bunch of different animals there, and they gave me a pile of scientific papers and told me to study them. A couple of those papers were about tapirs, and that is how I learned about them. I learned about how they disperse seeds and are called the 'gardeners of the forest.' I thought that was extremely interesting and thought, 'Wow, this is such a great animal.'" But it would be a while before tapirs became Medici's life's work.

Eventually, Medici began working with a married couple who were a primatologist and an environmental educator, taking time to help them in the field during her vacations from school. This helped her build her career in wildlife ecology and conservation. Later, she and the couple, along with half a dozen others, would go on to found Instituto de Pesquisas Ecológicas (Institute for Ecological Research) in Brazil. That's when the semi-serendipity struck.

"We were celebrating together because we had just gotten the official document that said our institute formally existed," Medici explains. "Now that we had the institute, we had to decide what we were going to do with it. We wanted to focus on species conservation, so we made a list of animals we wanted to work with. We came up with three criteria for an animal to make the list: first, the animals had to be threatened with extinction; second, they had to be animals that people knew very little about; and third, they had to be so difficult to study that nobody else wanted to work with them. That's when I suggested the tapir because few people, including scientists, knew anything much about them because they are so difficult to study. So we put them on the list. And then a few years later, I got a grant to work exclusively with tapirs.

"When we finally got started with tapirs, it was supposed to be a small project that would last only a couple of years, but then it took over my life. When you do research, you get more questions than answers. While you're answering one question, dozens more questions arise. Then you start thinking about the gaps in the knowledge and the missing pieces of the puzzle. And while I do love tapirs and don't think I would want to work with any other animals at this point, my real passion is in finding those answers. People often ask me, 'Don't you have enough knowledge of tapirs now? Don't you want to work with another animal for a while?' And I always say no. Tapirs, for me, are a platform for everything else. I can use my work with them to do really good science, and the answers we find can apply to helping other animals, too."

[NOTE TO SELF

When she looks back on how responsible and independent she was as a child, Medici has an interesting take on things: "When you're that focused that young, you don't enjoy certain parts of your life," she says. "Sometimes I think I didn't enjoy being a kid enough. I was always first in my class. When we finally got to college, my friends would tease me—in a friendly way—by saying things like 'Hey, here comes the top student!' So I remember a conversation I had with my mom one day over lunch, after I got into college. I told her, 'Look, I was a nerd all my life. All my scores were perfect. Now I'm moving out. I'm not going to go off the deep end; you don't have to worry. But I'm going to try to enjoy life some. I may not always have the top scores every time, so be prepared for that.' And my mom, as usual, was so great. She told me, 'You deserve to enjoy life a little bit more.' Once I moved out to attend the university at the age of sixteen, I no longer had to help my mom with the house, the finances, and my brother. I was able to be a teenager and finally do some stupid things. And I don't regret that at all."

■ ■ ■

[NOTE TO YOU

Medici hopes you realize the unprecedented access to information that you have right at your fingertips. "Kids today have all this wonderful technology!" she says. "They have access to so many things we didn't when I was growing up! My daughter has had a little laptop next to mine since she was in elementary school. She could research anything, anytime. At the age of eight, she was researching sustainable development, sitting next to me, watching YouTube videos on the topic and learning all kinds of things. The world is a wealth of opportunities for kids today. I didn't feel like that when I was little: I had to fight for every piece of information and every opportunity."

Because technology now makes it so easy to reach out to others with your interests, Medici hopes you'll seize the opportunities afforded to you. "Now that we have email and all kinds of ways to network and contact potential mentors and coaches from all over the world, why wouldn't you? I take advantage of technology in this way now, and you can take advantage of it a lot earlier than I was able to in my studies."

[WORDS TO LIVE BY

When asked for her best advice, Medici shared what she tells her own children. Of course, she speaks Portuguese to them, but she gave it a go in English just for you! "I guess you could translate it as 'Don't do to others what you wouldn't want done to you,'" she says. "That means be kind if you want kindness from others. Be ethical if you want to be treated ethically. I'm very careful about being the kind of person I want people to be with me."

MEET THE TAPIRS

ITS BODY IS SORT OF like a pig's. Its snout is kind of a cross between an anteater's and an elephant's, but shorter. The tapir (pronounced just like the word "taper") is a mammal you may never have seen before in real life, unless you live in South or Central America or Southeast Asia. In Belize, where tapirs are the official national animal, they're called "mountain cows." However, tapirs are not actually cows, but rather cousins of horses and rhinoceroses.

The most distinguishing aspect of the tapir is its unusual snout. Its nose sort of hangs down over its mouth, but not as far as an elephant's trunk. However, this almost-trunk is flexible like an elephant's and is quite useful for grabbing vegetation. (Unlike anteaters, tapirs are herbivores, so they don't eat ants, and they certainly won't eat you . . . unless you happen to be a fruit or vegetable, of course.)

The short, flexible trunk can also act as a sort of snorkel if the tapir has to hide in the water for a while to escape predators. Not to say that tapirs are pushovers. They are highly aggressive and territorial when threatened and more likely to attack than to run away. Of course, you probably wouldn't want to threaten them: tapirs have sharp teeth and are pretty massive—they can weigh up to about seven hundred pounds (three hundred kilograms)!

Conservationists want to save tapirs, not just because they should have a right to exist, but also because they perform an important task in the ecosystem: they poop. We know—that doesn't seem like such a big deal. After all, everyone you've ever met has been pooping their whole lives and nobody's given them an award for it, right? But tapir poop is special. You see, because tapirs eat all those fruits, vegetables, and leaves, their waste contains seeds and vital nutrients that help keep plants growing in different areas. When tapirs simply wander around and use the bathroom wherever they may be, they aid in spreading seeds and also help the soil stay rich. That's why they're called the "gardeners of the forests." Just by pooping, tapirs are doing important ecological work. (And to think, you have to actually clean your room and do your homework to feel appreciated!)

Despite their substantial size and their kind of gross-to-talk-about job, the more you look at tapirs, the cuter they seem. When they're babies, they have adorable stripes and spots to help camouflage them, but those markings fade away as they grow up. Another oddly endearing trait of tapirs is their high-pitched form of communication with one another. If you've ever let the air out of a balloon slowly such that it makes a whistling noise, then you have some idea of how a tapir sounds— probably not the noise you would've expected to come from these hefty mammals! Tapirs are highly intelligent animals and can be affectionate in captivity, but don't try to adopt one because, let's be honest, they'd rather be out doing their thing, and we need them out there doing all that important, *ahem* . . . gardening.

Unfortunately, tapirs, like so many other animals, are a threatened species because humans continue to hunt them and destroy their habitat. Tapirs are not born in litters like puppies or kittens: a mama tapir is pregnant for thirteen months before she delivers a single calf, which will likely live about twenty-five years (unless it's killed by a hunter or predator, hit by a car, or starved after its habitat has been turned into a parking lot or what-have-you). Some people actually eat tapirs, which makes about as much sense as eating a panda or a snow leopard. When a species is on the verge of extinction, wouldn't it make more sense to just have a salad?

So if you ever see tapirs, give 'em a high five! Well, maybe a high four instead. Tapirs have four toes on their front hooves and three toes on their back ones. They're the only animals native to their habitat that have this distinction, because, hey, they're cool like that. Also, the spacing of their toes helps them walk better in mud, so there's that. But since they are big, wild animals with sharp teeth, maybe you could just skip the high five and appreciate them from afar. That sounds like a better plan.

DAVA NEWMAN

Rethinking the Marshmallow Space Suit

As an aerospace biomedical engineer and former NASA deputy administrator, Professor Dava Newman of MIT has a list of accomplishments and awards that might be as long as this book, but what she's most known for is thinking about what to wear—no, not for a big party or for yearbook picture day, but for a trip to Mars!

When you think of space suits, you probably think of what's commonly known as balloon suits, those puffy white ones that make astronauts look like marshmallow people, complete with goldfish bowls on top of their heads. This suit, standard pretty much since the beginning of the space program, was the best technology going for years, and even though it wasn't the hippest look, it had a job to do. You see, a space suit is basically a spacecraft an astronaut wears. You can't exactly rocket to the moon and expect to walk around in jeans and a T-shirt. The space suit allowed astronauts to move around while protecting them from the vacuum of space, insulating them from the extreme temperatures and radiation, and providing them oxygen to breathe. Oh, and it also kept them from getting banged up from space dust, which doesn't sound all that dangerous but is basically space debris whizzing by at bullet speed. Ouch.

One of the main jobs of the space suit has always been to provide pressure on the astronaut's body. (See page 75 to find out why.) The old balloon suit provided gas pressurization, but its puffy structure had some limitations.

First of all, the traditional suit is pretty rigid. When those balloons suits blow up, it can be tough to move around in them—kind of like when your mom bundles you up in several layers before you go out and play in the snow, and your arms and legs are so hard to bend that you can barely manage to pack together a decent snowball. And let's be honest, doing repairs on space stations and space shuttles is much more involved than a snowball fight. So you can see why it was time for an upgrade.

Newman's BioSuit looks less like a marshmallow and more like something a modern superhero would wear. It's skintight and has all sorts of cool fibers running along it.

Besides applying pressure and allowing for greater movement, the BioSuit will keep astronauts from having to worry about their balloon suits being "popped" by the space debris whizzing by them.

You know what else is awesome about the BioSuit? Putting it on! Not just because it's cool, but because it's functional. The traditional balloon suit was too bulky for astronauts to put on by themselves; they had to have help. But since astronauts can put on the BioSuit independently, they're able to save valuable time. (It's going to cost a lot of money to get people to Mars, so when we get them there, we need them to be as efficient as possible.)

The BioSuit sounds so awesome that you may be wondering why NASA didn't just use a suit like it to begin with. But keep in mind that when the original space suit was designed, modern fabrics such as spandex didn't even exist. Of course, there are other considerations besides just the tightness: Newman's team is working to simplify the traditional space suit's life-support system, known as the backpack, which provides oxygen and thermal control that astronauts need in space. They're attempting to create something more like what deep-sea divers use. And they designed a smaller helmet that allows astronauts to turn their heads, which is impossible in the traditional space suit design.

The BioSuit has amazing potential here on Earth, too.

Eventually, the fibers running along the suit may be able to be fitted with electrodes that can stimulate movement. For stroke victims, people with cerebral palsy, or infants with brain damage, this might help reshape their motor programs and improve their mobility. Over time, movement signals that are sent to the brain may retrain it to produce movement on its own. The Bio-Suit, though designed for a trip to the moon or Mars, may revolutionize medical treatment for patients who previously had little hope for increased motor control.

So how did a girl from Helena, Montana, grow up to change the way we envision astronauts and potentially revolutionize medical treatment for mobility impairments?

[THE SPARK

Newman's parents were both teachers, so she grew up loving to learn. Her dad later became a congressional campaign manager, so their family kept up with the news. Newman clearly recalls

watching the coverage of the Apollo 11 space mission when she was about five years old. "We were in our den, watching TV. I understood that President Kennedy was sending us to the moon, and it taught me to dream. Also, I was in the perfect place to dream, because there's no better place than Montana to watch the night sky." Did that view of the sky make young Dava want to become an astronaut? Nope. "At that age, I wanted to be president!" she says.

Dava and her two older brothers "grew up running around in mountains and caves," she says. "I tagged along to everything." Their parents gave them plenty of independence. "We played outside all the time, and my parents just knew we were somewhere," she explains. Having two big brothers who loved sports fueled her interest in athletics, and Dava played every sport in school, her favorites being basketball and ski racing. "I had a stuffed monkey, but other than that, my toys were all the sporting equipment anyone could have," says Newman.

When Dava was twelve, her parents divorced, and she took her first job, working at a root beer stand. "Then I decided to start my own business so I could set my own hours and play basketball every morning at 6 a.m.," she says. "I became a shoe-shine girl. I shined a lot of cowboy boots in Montana!"

Not surprisingly, Dava loved school. "I liked all subjects. But if you did well in math, they let you run the school store and sell candy, so that was a positive reward for being good in math in fifth grade. Still, my family was more into the humanities, so I loved creative writing and philosophy as well. I had great math teachers but also an exceptional creative writing teacher." At Dava's public school, AP courses were not offered at the time. "Mr. Bozdog, my math teacher, told me to learn calculus, even though it wasn't a course option. He gave us extra problems to work and was always pushing us to the next level."

Upon graduation from high school, Dava was offered an appointment to West Point Military Academy. "I had no money, and every adult I knew said, 'Do it; it's paid for,'" she says.

"But in my heart, it didn't feel right for me. Instead, I did an Army/ROTC fellowship to Notre Dame for the first year and a half, and after that I relied on academic scholarships and working my way through college." Dava began as a prelaw major, intending to become a sports lawyer. "But I was completely bored by case law," she explains. "My brother Brad, a lawyer himself, gave me great advice when he said, 'Dava, with your math and science abilities, you could do something technical.' There wasn't a single person in my immediate family in the technology field, but I changed my major during my freshman year of college. My uncle Bill, who lived in Seattle, was a bioengineer, and the thought of helping people inspired me. I had to catch up during my sophomore year to get into the aerospace engineering program." It turned out to be a perfect fit. "It was natural for me to think about physics and things like parabolic trajectories because of all my sports training," says Newman. "The connection between that kind of thinking and basketball, golf, softball, and ski racing is actually huge, although I didn't realize it then. I ended up specializing in biomechanics, and sports is all about that. I later went to MIT for graduate school to specialize in astronaut performance."

[THE EUREKA MOMENT

Newman now has four suit designs and five patents, although the BioSuit is the one that gets the most publicity. "My specialty is understanding astronauts and how they perform in reduced gravity," she says. "I spent a decade designing space suits and studying astronaut movement and trying to enhance flexibility." But it was when she took a vacation that her eureka moment really occurred. In 2002–2003, she spent eighteen months sailing around the entire world with her husband and business partner, Guillermo Trotti. On the sailboat, Newman found herself with a lot of time to think. She began pondering counterpressure and the idea of applying pressure directly to the skin from the space suit. "The time on the boat made me think, 'How can we do this differently?'" she says. "Either you put someone in a balloon suit, or you apply pressure directly to the skin. I had studied the work of Dr. Paul Webb and Dr. Arthur Iberall. Webb designed a space activity suit, and he thought in terms of tight instead of big, and I thought maybe he'd had a great idea way before its time. Iberall had an interesting idea on patterning a space suit to make it more flexible." While still on the boat, Dava transformed these early ideas and wrote her proposal to NASA for what would become the BioSuit.

[NOTE TO SELF

When asked what advice Newman would give her younger self, she didn't hesitate. "Dream big!" she says. "No dream is too big. Don't listen to 'no.' The answer is always 'yes' because young people are infinitely creative. See yourself in the role you want and know that you belong and know that we need you in STEM. I've been told many times that I have crazy ideas, that it can't be done. I've been told that a lot, especially about the BioSuit. But I keep going forward. I'd tell my young self to keep playing all those sports, too, because it taught me to compete harder and keep on going, and I learned how to accept failure. I learned leadership and discipline. Yes, I'd definitely tell her to keep with the sports!"

. . .

[NOTE TO YOU

Newman thinks it's important that we change the conversation around STEM. "I prefer to call it STEAMD because the arts and design are so important," she says. "We need to reach across disciplines and be inclusive. Many STEM programs try to 'weed people out,' but I think it does profound damage to weed out all that potential. You don't have to be the best at calculus and physics and math—those are just tools we use, but they're not everything. Take those hard classes, yes, but more important, just decide what you want to do and say yes to yourself. Everyone has infinite potential, in infinite combinations! Everyone is smart and unique. Ask yourself, 'What's the most important problem I can address today?' and work hard. Be persistent."

[WORDS TO LIVE BY

"My philosophy is this: Love, Act, Discover, and Innovate. It makes a great acronym, 'LADI,' pronounced like 'lady.' I came up with it in my teaching to share with my students, and it's been invaluable to me in my career, too."

WHY IS IT SO IMPORTANT FOR A SUIT TO PROVIDE PRESSURE, ANYWAY?

HAS YOUR FOOT (or hand or arm or leg or any body part) ever "fallen asleep"? You know . . . that weird tingly feeling you get when you stay in an odd position too long and your blood circulation to that area is limited, followed by the feeling of being gently stabbed with a thousand needles as the blood rushes back to that area? Well, if you've had this experience (and who hasn't?), then you know a little something about the effects of pressure on the human body.

Blood circulation has a lot to do with pressure. That pressure can come in the form of sitting on your foot too long or even taking a plane trip. You may have heard of compression socks or tights. Often, elderly people and others with circulatory issues wear these on planes because as the plane goes up in the sky, air pressure decreases. The socks and tights make up for this decrease in air pressure by applying pressure to the legs so that the wearer's blood has an easier time circulating back upward instead of pooling in their ankles. Space suits do sort of the same thing for astronauts, except all over their bodies—and for a longer period of time. For example, it will take about eight months to get to Mars; then astronauts will explore the planet for six hundred days, looking for the evidence of life (past or present); and then it will take more than twelve months to return to Earth. A big trip for sure, but Mars is, after all, approximately 140 million miles (225 million kilometers) away!

A lack of pressure can do all kinds of funky stuff to the human body besides decreasing circulation. For one thing, when pressure drops, so does a liquid's boiling point. That means that without a space suit's pressure control, astronauts' blood would literally start boiling! How gross is that?

But changes in pressure can cause subtler side effects as well. If you've ever gotten elevation sickness, you've experienced some of these effects. Say you climb a mountain. As you get higher up, the pressure drops, so the oxygen molecules spread out more. This affects your organs, especially your brain and lungs. You may have trouble breathing, and you may develop a headache or nausea if you don't have enough oxygen. Now just imagine those same kinds of effects, only much higher up in space instead of on a mountain.

In space, one of the biggest concerns is how the reduced gravity affects the muscles and bones. Astronauts experience a 40 percent reduction in their muscle strength and a significant reduction in their bone density (1 to 2 percent reduction per month) due to the weak gravity of space. How does this happen?

Well, you may not realize it, but your bones are alive! They are constantly repairing themselves and replacing old bone tissue with new bone tissue. If you're young and healthy, your bones replace the old stuff with the new stuff at the same time, and you never even know it's happening. But when you get older, that process slows down, which is why you may have noticed that older people tend to have more bone trouble. The lack of gravity in space affects astronauts' bones in a similar way: the microgravity slows down the new bone production, so it's almost like their bones become much older in a short amount of time. In fact, astronauts' bones may not feel normal again for three or four years after they return to Earth.

Pressurized space suits are so important because they somewhat mimic the pressure and atmosphere that our bodies need to live here on Earth. Pressure and gravity are both necessary to help the body's muscles, bones, and circulatory and nervous systems perform more like they do on our home planet.

And, you know, pressure keeps the astronauts' blood from boiling, which the astronauts totally appreciate.

MAUREEN RAYMO

Unlocking Climate Change Secrets from
the Earth and the Ocean

Dr. Maureen Raymo has a job that many small children would
envy: she digs around in the mud. Lots of mud. But no mud pies
are involved because Raymo isn't so much interested in the mud
itself—it's what she might find in it. Her job involves going out
to sea on big boats that are equipped with huge drills. They use

these drills to bring up stacks of mud, or what scientists call "sediment cores," so they can analyze what's inside. (More on that in a minute.)

Raymo is a paleoclimatologist, which is a very big word for a very big field of study. Her job is to study Earth's history to try and figure out what caused climate changes in the past. That information can then be used to predict climate changes in our planet's future. Digging through the deep-sea sediments provides historical data that help scientists create and test climate models that can be used to predict Earth's future—sort of an extremely advanced weather report.

Unless you've been living under a rock (please enjoy that geology pun), you've probably heard about global warming. To understand the implications of global warming, it's important to understand global cooling as well. Scientists believe that for the most part, Earth has been pretty warm throughout its history. But like the weather, Earth's climate is highly variable over long time periods. At some points in the planet's history, it's as though someone cranked up the AC, resulting in periods of time known as ice ages, when huge sheets of ice formed in places like Antarctica and Greenland.

Scientists have shown that the cause of periodic ice ages is changes in the pattern of Earth's orbit around the sun, the source of our heat. These climate cycles are called Milankovitch cycles after the person who first made calculations about how Earth's orbit varied over thousands of years.

Scientists theorize that the Earth's climate also varies on even longer, million year timescales. In 1989, Raymo presented an idea that got the attention of everyone in the scientific community: she proposed that the formation of the Himalayas, the greatest mountain range in the world, may have caused the overall global cooling that led to the growth of the Antarctic ice sheet about forty million years ago.

The Himalayas formed when the two landmasses of India and Asia collided with each other. Continents ride on tectonic plates, large segments of Earth's outer shell that are continuously moving on Earth's surface. When plates spread apart, carbon dioxide (CO_2) escapes from Earth's interior in the form of volcanic gases; when the plates collide, mountains form, and the atmospheric CO_2 is absorbed by erosion and weathering in the mountains.

Raymo's proposal, known as the Uplift-Weathering Hypothesis, is based on what you've probably heard about global warming—that carbon dioxide causes Earth to heat up. The more CO_2 you have in the atmosphere, the warmer the planet is, so it made sense to Raymo that when the Himalayas formed and absorbed CO_2, Earth's temperature dropped. In Raymo's own words, the Himalayas "are like a huge sponge pulling CO_2 out of the atmosphere. I think these mountains are in large part responsible for all of the global cooling of the last forty million years."

Now's the part where we get back to all that mud. When CO_2 levels change, so do sea levels. That is because as it gets colder, polar ice sheets grow and take water out of the ocean—and when climate warms, ice sheets melt and put the water back in the ocean. Raymo studies the link between CO_2 change and the pattern of ice growth and decay in the past by studying fossils from the deep sea. As Raymo herself explains it, "If you think about the ocean, it's like a giant bucket. All the mud that washes in from rivers, all the fossil shells of plankton that live and die in the surface ocean, all the dust that blows in from the air . . . it all falls to the bottom of the ocean. All this material from land and sea accumulates layer by layer over thousands of years. We can go out on a ship to the middle of the ocean and recover a long sediment core. If you had a layer cake and you put a clear straw in the middle of it and then pulled the straw back up, you could see the history of how that cake was made by looking at its layers. That's essentially what we're doing with ocean sediment, but we're looking at the Earth's history in those layers. How much dust was blown in from land? How much volcanic ash was there? How did sea level and ice volume change? It's like a timeline of history."

The drillship *JOIDES Resolution*

So how did a little girl born in Los Angeles wind up in the middle of the ocean as chief scientist on a giant drillship? It may have had something to do with a TV show!

[THE SPARK

Although she was born in Los Angeles, Maureen's family moved to Massachusetts when her father took a job as a physics and astronomy professor at a college there. He also wrote a science column for a Boston newspaper. With a science professor father and a mother who was a special education teacher, Maureen grew up in a household that valued learning—and independence. Maureen and her three younger siblings had, as she recalls, "tons of freedom." She fondly remembers "roaming the woods and meadows for hours and riding our bikes for miles." But it was a television show that may have really inspired her.

"Oceanographer Jacques Cousteau had a TV show back then, when I was about seven years old," Raymo says. "It was called *The Undersea World of Jacques Cousteau*, and I wanted to be an oceanographer just like him."

Besides the inspiration from Cousteau, Raymo also thinks that being the oldest child may have greatly shaped who she became. "Maybe it's some sort of 'first-child overachiever' thing. I just know that my parents always told me I could be anything I wanted to be. They never said, 'You can't do that.'" Another thing Raymo credits with building her leadership skills and courage? Girl Scouts. "That was a big part of my life," she says. "I was a Girl Scout from the time I was seven till I was eighteen."

As far as her STEM beginnings, Raymo says she "definitely was not a child prodigy" but was good at science and math. In those days, she says, being a girl who excelled in STEM "meant

you were a geek; it meant you were bullied." For that reason, school wasn't a fun place for Maureen. While she says she was "average" at her chosen school sports, field hockey and basketball, Maureen otherwise didn't really enjoy school. Luckily, her family and Girl Scouts were able to expose her to a much larger world, where she found a lot to get excited about.

"I always knew I wanted to explore. Always," she says. "I was crazy about travel. My parents traveled with us a lot. When I was eight, we lived in England for a year while my dad was on sabbatical [time off professors get from their colleges/universities to devote to intense study]. Another time he was on sabbatical, when I was twelve, we lived in a small fishing village in Ireland. I just always liked roaming the coastline."

Raymo says she continued her parents' methods with her own children. "I kind of adapted their 'benign neglect' theory of child rearing and let them have room to explore and also took them to see different parts of the world. It's good for kids to see different ways of living. My son and I lived in India for three months when he was in high school. I dragged my kids everywhere!"

As a senior in high school, Maureen wound up being the only student in her class to be accepted at an Ivy League school. Still in love with oceanography, Maureen went to Brown University, ready to begin studying science and continue exploring. Brown had a program in marine geoscience, which combined oceanography and geology—a program few schools had. An internship with a paleoclimatology professor helped Maureen find what would become her life's work. She earned her PhD from Columbia University, where she is now a professor, and has been studying and exploring ever since.

[THE EUREKA MOMENT

Some eureka moments for scientists come in expected ways, like from working with other scientists or sharing ideas with them. This happened to Raymo when she was a graduate student attending an international meeting. "Another graduate student presented some data that helped me connect the dots on what would become the uplift hypothesis," she recalls. "I thought, 'Oh, wow, this is the missing piece of the puzzle!'" The other student's data allowed Raymo to return to her work with new insights that would help her formulate and clarify her own hypothesis.

Other eureka moments are more serendipitous. While a TV show helped young Maureen find her passion, a movie lent Raymo some critical inspiration later in her career. "I watched a movie called *March of the Penguins*," she says. "It was about how these penguins from Antarctica travel to their breeding grounds to mate, so they have to march across the tundra. And I went to sleep and dreamed about it. In my dream, they were marching through a meadow. When I woke up, I thought, 'Maybe there was a time in history when Antarctica wasn't covered in ice.' It made me think about different ways Antarctica could have looked in the past, which led to further study about climate change. So you never know where inspiration will come from!"

[NOTE TO SELF

If she could talk to her younger self, Raymo says she'd tell her just three things: "Hang in there. You can do anything. Be confident in yourself."

[NOTE TO YOU

"I'd tell any kid that any amazing, exciting life you can dream, you can live," Raymo says. "Be ambitious. Think big." While she thinks studying is important, she also thinks it's important to do things that just make you happy. "My daughter has a PhD in economics, and my son has a degree in geology and works for the International Ocean Discovery Program in College Station, Texas," she says. "But I wasn't always pushing academics. When my son wanted to go to skateboard camp, I was fine with it."

And while you're thinking big and pursuing happiness, Raymo would greatly appreciate it if you'd do everything you can to limit carbon dioxide emissions. "While some of the changes in carbon dioxide are caused by big events like mountains forming or volcanoes erupting, most of today's warming is caused by human activity," she explains. "As CO_2 levels continue to rise, the Earth will continue to warm, the ice at the poles will continue to melt, and sea levels will continue to rise." Raymo cautions that this could mean some landmasses literally going under. So please, do your part to take good care of the environment. Turn the page for more info on ways you can help.

[WORDS TO LIVE BY

Fun fact: even brilliant scientists have inspirational quotations on their fridge! On Raymo's fridge are the words "Create Your Perfect Day, Every Day," and she says she does think about that daily. "The key word there is 'create,'" she explains. "It's your choice. You can create something wonderful every day of your life. Even if it is just peacefulness."

CAN WE REALLY SAVE THE EARTH?

IF YOU THINK OF EARTH as our home, we have a pretty big family: about seven and a half billion humans currently live on this planet together! Earth scientists like Maureen Raymo study how our home works, and they urge us to clean up whatever messes we make to keep it nice. "If your refrigerator breaks, you fix it, because you take care of the things you need and care about," Raymo says. "In a similar way, our planet currently needs fixing because of the problem we're having with climate change."

Raymo says that the burning of fossil fuels is polluting the atmosphere with massive amounts of carbon dioxide, and that this is a major factor in causing Earth's temperature to rise. "We can't ignore that humans are causing this pollution in our atmosphere and in our oceans," she says. "Even though you can't see it or smell it, carbon dioxide is a waste product, and it's causing the Earth to heat up, the ice sheets to melt, and the seas to rise. This will threaten the lives and homes of the hundreds of millions of people who live near the ocean."

You've probably heard plenty of ways we can all make a difference, but are you doing them? One way you can help, according to Raymo, is by doing something your parents have been begging you to do for years: eat your veggies! Raymo has said that cutting down on beef consumption and opting instead for chicken, pork, and vegetables is "one of the most impactful things you can do right away" to make a difference in the environment because raising cattle uses far more water, fertilizer, and land, and releases far more CO_2 than the farm production of other forms of protein and nutrition.

Here are some other steps you can take to do your part!

MAREENA ROBINSON SNOWDEN

Using Science for World Peace

Nuclear warheads, as you probably know, are some of the most destructive weapons on earth, with the capacity to kill millions of people at once. Countries that have nuclear weapons, therefore, are kind of like the toughest kids in school: nobody wants to mess with them. But having those weapons is dangerous, and knowing that another country has those weapons can make conflict fraught with hostility and fear. So when peace treaties are made, countries can sign agreements to disarm their nuclear weapons—in other words, to get rid of or disable some or all of their weapons so that they can't be used anymore. It's a way of saying, "Hey, let's be friends or at least not kill each other." But it's one thing to say you're going to disarm your weapons and another to actually *do* it. How do we know when a country that makes such a promise actually follows through?

Hmmm . . . If only there were some way to assess nuclear weapons to make sure they'd been disarmed. If only some super-smart scientist were working on how to do that, wouldn't that be, well . . . super? Wouldn't we totally put her in this book?

Yes! Yes, we would!

Meet super-smart scientist Dr. Mareena Robinson Snowden. Not only did she make history by becoming the first African American woman to receive a PhD in nuclear science and engineering from MIT, but she also tackled the question of how to confirm that nuclear disarmament actually happens. Cool, right? The people at Marvel Comics thought so. Yes, Robinson Snowden is featured in an actual Marvel comic! (*The Unstoppable Wasp* #6, if you want to check it out.) Guess it's safe to say we're not the only ones who think she's a superhero!

How did Robinson Snowden grow up to make history and potentially help secure world peace? It all started generations before Mareena herself was born in Miami, Florida.

[THE SPARK

"I've never been one to hold a pity party for myself when things didn't go my way," Robinson Snowden says. "I learned that from my family, especially my dad." Mareena's parents divorced when she was only four, and her father raised her and her sisters as a single parent. "Dad was like, 'If you fall off your bike, get back up,'" she recalls. In fact, Mareena comes from a long line of people who believed in personal perseverance. Mareena's grandparents were the children of farmers and sharecroppers (people who farm land they don't own in exchange for a place to live and a portion of the crops), but amazingly, four of her great-uncles got their PhDs in the 1950s and '60s, when segregation laws deprived Black Americans of many of their basic rights as citizens. "My uncles couldn't drink at the [whites-only-designated] water fountain, but they were getting their PhDs," Robinson Snowden marvels. "And my great-grandparents picked cotton. Understanding this legacy that spanned from the cotton fields to the highest levels of academia gives me a tremendous amount of pride. It helps to contextualize whatever hardships I endure, and I can assure you they are nothing compared to what my family has overcome."

This family pride runs deep in Robinson Snowden's family and has much to do with her success. It was Mareena's grandmother who convinced her to accept a slot at an elite math and science academy, even though Mareena wanted to stay at her regular school, where she was on the track team and had a boyfriend. "I put up a very strong resistance," Robinson Snowden says. "But my grandmother got down on her knees and begged me to go. You can't say no to your grandma!" So Mareena went, even though the commute meant leaving her house every morning at five o'clock and catching two buses and a train.

Robinson Snowden also credits her family with developing her self-esteem so that she had the confidence to pursue such a challenging curriculum. When she was a little girl, she'd go on car rides with her grandfather, who allowed her to ask questions about anything that interested her. The catch was that she had to ask follow-up questions as well. "This has been so helpful to me as an adult," she explains, "because it helped me learn how to form a question and a follow-up question and get to the 'why.' A lot of my work as an engineer is about the 'why.' To this day, I'm not satisfied if I don't understand the 'why' of what I'm working on." Mareena's questions (which were usually about her family history, a topic she found fascinating) pleased her grandfather, who always praised her with the words "You have a good mind."

Another skill her father and grandfather helped Mareena with? Public speaking.

"Every Sunday after church, we'd go to the Piccadilly café, and my dad would make me stand up and give a speech!" Mareena says. "I quickly figured out the talking points that would get my granddaddy excited—anything about my education. So I'd stand up in the middle of the restaurant and announce, 'I want to go to Harvard or Yale,' and give a speech on that. It taught me to get over my nerves and say something substantive. We didn't know that I'd wind up becoming a nuclear engineer who would have to do exactly that in order to give presentations."

You might think that with all this family support, growing up was a breeze for Mareena. Not so much. "I wasn't the coolest kid," she says. "I had friends, but I wasn't the girl with the latest clothes and shoes. I often wore my sister's hand-me-downs because my father didn't value the latest Nikes and Jordans the way middle schoolers did, nor did he have the extra money to spend on those things. But he made sure I was involved in sports, so I did karate and soccer when I was little. My sister and I were the only girls on the seven- to nine-year-olds' soccer team, but I didn't even realize it at the time. All I knew was that my dad taught me not to sit on the sidelines, but to get in the game. In middle school, I ran track and continued that in high school along with the swim team. I wasn't great at either sport, but I kept up."

Surprisingly, Mareena wasn't known as "the brain," either. "I did my schoolwork," she says, "and I was a good student, but my favorite subjects were PE and lunch! I preferred English and history and didn't really get into science until tenth grade. That's when I had wonderful teachers who reframed my fear of science and math. Most teachers seemed to have a preconceived idea of who the 'STEM people' were—the ones who got it immediately. That wasn't me. I wasn't a 'natural'; I had to work for it. But Ms. Biscombe, my Algebra II teacher, saw each student as capable. She was so creative and would make up rap songs about derivatives, and she would give as many sample problems as I needed. She'd stay after school to answer my questions. Ms. Biscombe always made me feel that I was capable. Before her class, I'd never gotten excited about math because I was afraid of getting the wrong answer, but she would always help me rethink problems to figure out where I'd gone wrong.

"Another teacher who helped me love STEM was Dr. Khalil, my physics teacher in twelfth grade. She was so organized and methodical. She gave the steps! I LOVE steps! If I know the steps, I can get the answer. Dr. Khalil challenged the way I saw science by demystifying it into a series of steps that can be followed."

In spite of those experiences with science and math, when it was time for college, Mareena planned to study business at Florida A&M University (FAMU) and then become an attorney like her father. But when they visited campus, things changed. Big time.

Mareena's dad knew someone in the physics department at FAMU, so they stopped by. What she didn't know was that it was so hard to get people to major in physics that the department rolled out the red carpet to any potential candidates. "They treated me like a football star!" Robinson Snowden recalls. Her dad was so confident in Mareena—and in what a physics degree could mean for her—that he asked her to give it a try. "The plan was that I could change majors if I didn't like it," she recalls. "But the next thing you know, I look up and I'm a junior!"

[THE EUREKA MOMENT

Robinson Snowden insists that her real discovery was more about herself than about nuclear disarmament. When she decided to continue her STEM education in graduate school, her school offered three specialties in nuclear engineering: fission, fusion, or nuclear science and technology. (What's the diff? See page 102.) Mareena chose fusion. However, during her first semester, she kept hearing on the news about the nuclear program in Iran. "Negotiations between our country and Iran had started years before, and the people on the news were talking about noncompliance," Robinson Snowden explains. "I had never thought much about nuclear weapons, but I knew there was a course about nuclear nonproliferation being offered, so because of the news, I was kind of interested. I enrolled in the course, and pretty soon, I was so engrossed in the topic that I changed my research focus to monitoring nuclear warheads by the radiation they emit. The fuel that drives a nuclear explosion is radioactive—these warheads emit their own radiation. So it's an energy question: How energetic is this radiation? You can use the energy of the gamma ray to see how it was generated and also from what materials it was generated."

Even if you haven't studied radiation, you probably know that it exists all over the place and in many forms. Your sunblock protects you from ultraviolet radiation; your microwave cooks your food using radiation (hence the slang "nuking" your food). But most people aren't terrified of walking outside or zapping a pizza. That's because not all radiation is created equal. Radiation actually comes in seven different frequencies: radio waves, microwaves, infrared radiation, visible light, ultraviolet radiation, X-rays, and gamma rays. Some of these waves are dangerous, and some are relatively harmless. It all depends on where the frequencies fall on the radiation spectrum.

THE ELECTROMAGNETIC SPECTRUM

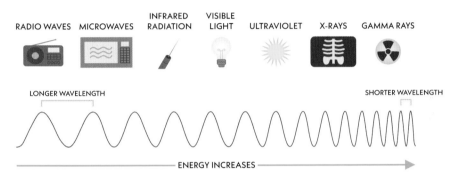

Your microwave, for example, won't make your food radioactive because it uses—you guessed it!—microwaves, which are at the lower end of the electromagnetic spectrum. It would take a lot of exposure to lower-end radiation to do real damage, which is why you wouldn't want to cook yourself in the sun for hours on end, climb into a microwave to warm up, or get an X-ray every week (though occasional X-rays are fine). Gamma rays, meanwhile, are the heavy hitters of the electromagnetic spectrum because of their high energy. They can do a lot of damage in a short time, which is one reason nuclear bombs are so destructive.

Nuclear warheads are designed with radioactive fuel and high explosives, which are responsible for detonation. Robinson Snowden's research focuses on identifying neutron sources (nuclear fuel) and high explosives together in a package. "This combination would be highly unlikely outside of a military context," she explains. "So the interaction of those materials is a reliable signal for the presence of a nuclear warhead."

A country that has this dangerous fuel-plus-explosives combo but claims not to have active warheads might as well claim to have peanut butter, jelly, and bread, but no sandwich. That's why this technology, in theory, allows inspectors to know whether or not countries are fibbing about dismantling their weapons.

To understand how Robinson Snowden's experiments work, we need to review a little bit about the structure of the atom. You probably know that atoms are made up of protons and neutrons (which together make up the atom's nucleus) and electrons. An atom of a given element (like carbon) has a set number of protons, but it can have different numbers of neutrons, and each version of the atom is called an isotope. Some of those isotopes are stable, which means that they won't change unless something external causes them to change, and some are unstable, which means they change over time on their own. (You may have heard of carbon-14, which archaeologists use to date fossils. Carbon-14 is an unstable isotope, or radioisotope, of the element carbon.)

In order to determine which materials are inside a warhead, Robinson Snowden leverages the fact that some isotopes inside the nuclear fuel are unstable. These isotopes can spontaneously release neutrons and split into two smaller, more stable nuclei. When the released neutrons collide with the nuclei of other material, say the surrounding explosive, those nuclei become "excited," which means that their energy level is increased. (Hey, if you were bombarded with neutrons, you'd probably be excited, too!) This extra energy in the nuclei has to go somewhere, so it's expelled in the form of gamma rays, which can be measured to help determine what the original substance was.

Yes, it's pretty complex, and it involves some fancy footwork to figure out exactly what's inside a warhead. Hey, no one said that world peace would be easy. But Robinson Snowden can't imagine working on anything else. When she realized that she was thinking and reading about nuclear disarmament in her free time, she knew she'd found her passion. "What I love about nuclear security," she explains, "is that it's interdisciplinary. It's not just a technical problem. It's cultural, it's policy-driven . . . All these things collide and are ultimately influenced by the politics of the time. Because I'd grown up with a love of history, I was also intrigued by how history has shaped who has nuclear weapons and how they got them. As an international community, it's been years and years of observing and trying to influence how the players in this chess game move their pieces on the board."

[NOTE TO SELF

"I wish I could tell my younger self, 'Hey, there are great things in your future!'" Robinson Snowden says. "I would tell her that God is moving in her life beyond anything she can even imagine, but that she has to be willing to stay the course, to do the work." She'd also remind her younger self to look past obstacles. "I'd tell myself, 'Tough times prepare you for the greatness that is beyond the hill, but you have to get to the top of the hill to see them,'" she says. "It's not a rosy road, and you will be knocked down, but you have to believe that the obstacles are there to teach you specific lessons and once you've mastered those lessons, that you will win. Also, remind yourself as an African American woman what your success means to your community. When I was younger, I didn't see any of this future for myself, but I was open to hard work and I think that was the most important thing."

She'd also tell her younger self not to be intimidated by other kids for whom STEM comes easily. "There were other students in my classes who 'got it' immediately, whatever the concept was," Robinson Snowden recalls. "That wasn't me. I absolutely hated those math problems that said things like 'It is intuitively obvious that . . .' or 'It can easily be derived . . .' because math wasn't intuitively obvious to me or easy for me to derive! I needed to see all the steps, and I still do! But we grow up with these narratives of people who are 'a natural,' and if you're not a natural, you think it's not for you. Well, natural talent is one thing, but nothing beats hard work! There are a lot of talented people who never realize their goals because they don't have the work ethic. Embrace the hard work because that is what will ultimately serve you."

[NOTE TO YOU

Robinson Snowden wants to tell you something important: "This is an amazing time to be alive!" she says. "The amount of information you have at your fingertips is unprecedented!" And so are the opportunities. She strongly suggests that you take advantage of summer STEM programs whenever possible. "Use that time to get into those communities," she urges. "It's not just about the skills, but the friends you make and the communities you become part of. That helps with success. A lot of these camps are free and they'll even fly you up there, but you have to be curious, diligent, and hardworking so that you make the most of the opportunity."

And when you're not at STEM camp or in the classroom? Try sports. "Sports can be a great way to learn how to lose and how to get back up," she says. "It's hard work. I remember running in the Miami heat, and it was hard! But I learned about rewards and I stayed physically fit." Robinson Snowden believes it's important not to spend too much time on video games on the internet. "The digital world is fun," she says, "but get outside! Get dirty! Mess up your hair! As a single parent, my father didn't raise us with the traditional gender norms that say little girls must be presentable at all times. He encouraged us to get out there, get dirty, and learn things. I wouldn't trade that freedom for anything."

Robinson Snowden would also like to talk to your parents and teachers about what they can do to help you. "Teachers and family members, be patient and supportive," she says. "In my case, I didn't show any aptitude for STEM until way late, but if my father had discouraged me from studying physics, none of this would have happened. The whole reason I switched to a science academy in high school was because my aunt found out about it and found out what I needed to do to apply and get in. And when I enrolled in physics in college, my dad believed I could do it if I worked and didn't try to take shortcuts. So lean in to your village and give kids opportunities, but also teach them to work and endure."

[WORDS TO LIVE BY

Robinson Snowden believes in memorizing and surrounding yourself with inspiring words. "When I was in grad school, my whole wall next to my desk was covered in scriptures," she says. "I also frequently recite the Lord's Prayer from memory when I'm nervous. Sometimes I'll be in a bathroom stall saying it in order to center myself, along with Ephesians 3:20–21, about how God will do abundantly more than what that we ask. And I always remember the story of Gideon from the book of Judges because it reminds me to hold fast to my faith.

"All this has sustained me and served me well," says Robinson Snowden. "God has a perfect track record in my life. Everything He has done has been for my development and His glory."

FISSION? FUSION? WHAT'S THE DIFF?

IN SIMPLEST TERMS, fission is the act of splitting something apart, while fusion is putting something together. (You may have seen the roots of these words in use before when someone describes a *fissure* in a rock or two ideas being *fused* into one—like fusion cuisine, where you might have teriyaki chicken in a taco. Yum!) But what do these words mean when it comes to nuclear technology?

In nuclear engineering, fission applies to splitting nuclei, and in short, it's what causes nuclear bombs to explode. When nuclei split, energy is released. Sometimes nuclei split naturally, but nuclear scientists can cause such a split to occur by artificial means so that the energy can be harnessed. This is called "controlled fission." Scientists purposely split an atom's nucleus into two smaller nuclei, which creates energy. Additionally, the neutrons that are emitted during the splitting of the nucleus emerge like rocks from a slingshot. Those neutrons bounce back and forth in the material, being absorbed by other nuclei and creating more fissions, which creates more neutrons. This process of one fission being caused by the neutrons from other is called a chain reaction, and results in a huge energy release. It's Energy City up in there! (Think of the released neutrons as many silver balls in an old pinball machine.) All this energy can be used to fuel nuclear power plants or nuclear weapons.

Fusion, on the other hand, is a reaction that powers the sun and other stars. Nuclear fusion occurs when light nuclei bond together to create heavier nuclei. Oddly enough, the mass of the new nuclei created in this process is actually less than the combined mass of the original two atoms. Where'd that extra mass go? It became energy! Most everybody has heard of Einstein's famous $E = mc^2$ formula, but few people know what it actually means. It's a mathematical representation of the relationship we just described: Energy equals mass times the speed of light squared. (We know . . . It seems weird that he used a c, but "celerity" is a big word scientists still sometimes use for speed. Now that you know what Einstein's formula stands for and what "celerity" means, it might be time to sign up for the Jeopardy! Teen Tournament.) Fusion is used in hydrogen bombs, but it also has the potential to create extremely clean energy with no radioactive waste in devices called fusion reactors, which would be extremely cool. (Feel free to grow up and become the scientist who perfects this! Our planet needs you!)

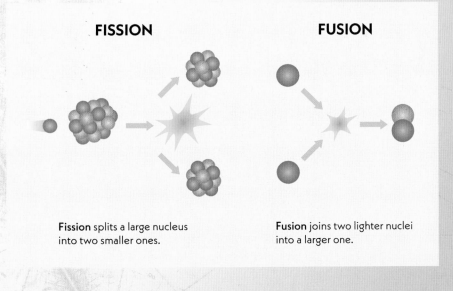

FISSION

FUSION

Fission splits a large nucleus into two smaller ones.

Fusion joins two lighter nuclei into a larger one.

MONSI ROMÁN

Cracking Down on the World's Tiniest Stowaways

[**FACT FILE**

Hometown: Guaynabo, Puerto Rico

Education: BS in Biology/Chemistry, Universidad de Puerto Rico, Río Piedras (1980); MS in Microbiology, University of Alabama in Huntsville (1991)

Employment: Program Manager/Microbiologist, NASA Marshall Space Flight Center

Top Honors and Achievements: NASA Silver Snoopy Award (2011); Hispanic Engineer National Achievement Awards Corporation Outstanding Technical Achievement – Government Award Winner (2012); NASA Innovation Award (2017)

When you think about the work NASA does, you probably think big: Rocket ships! Jet propulsion! Sonic booms! Giant leaps for humankind! And while all that stuff is undoubtedly way cool, chances are you haven't given much thought to the more minute details that go into a successful space project. And by "minute," we mean microscopic. Yes, when it comes to sending people and materials into space, NASA has to think of every detail . . . which is where microbiologist Monserrate (Monsi) Román comes in.

For more than thirty years now, Román has worked with NASA on big-time projects to keep small-time living things under control in the designing, building, and testing of life-support systems for space stations. One of the most important systems for the space station is the water recovery system (WRS), which includes water lines that bring clean water for drinking and remove wastewater to be cleaned. There are many complicated aspects about plumbing in space, but here's one you may not have thought about: stuff lives in water. And these small living things, called microorganisms or microbes, like to do what all living things like to do . . . grow and reproduce! That's why NASA has to be careful about how water is distributed, how long water sits in water lines without moving, and how to disinfect those lines. Lines that don't have water constantly flowing through them encourage microbe growth, and those microbes could grow and multiply and get into the astronauts' living quarters, where they could make them sick, or get into the space station's other parts and destroy components or cause something to break.

Microorganisms are capable of attaching to the surface of the water lines and producing a film that can protect them from disinfection. Because this film is made by living microbes, scientists refer to it as biofilm. Biofilms are found pretty much anywhere you have water and surfaces. And the thing about it, says Román, is that "microorganisms are really good at proliferating in there." Of course, there's biofilm on the plumbing lines where you live, too, but that's generally OK, because the Environmental Protection Agency controls the harmful microbes in your water with chemicals like chlorine and routinely monitors the water for your safety. If something goes wrong with your water, a quick call to the city water department or a plumber can take care of just about any issues. But when astronauts leave our atmosphere, they obviously can't call a plumber if something goes wrong.

"We have to make sure that in the spacecraft we control the bacteria that attaches to the surfaces," explains Román, "because they can create a mass that can make the astronauts sick and could also create mechanical problems." A space station's water lines are also a lot smaller than the ones in your home, so a blockage can happen a lot faster. That's why Román and her team have to make sure they're keeping everything as clean as possible. "I don't think you can prevent microbial growth entirely," Román explains. "There's biofilm in rivers, and that's what bacteria do, and they have a function. So I don't think you can entirely prevent them from colonizing surfaces. But if left unchecked, they can corrode the pipes and create holes or eat away at the sealants around the windows. So we control bacterial growth with iodine, and we use strong materials like titanium and stainless steel that have surfaces that will not corrode as easily when bacteria attach to them. And of course, we work very hard to prevent contamination at all levels."

Bacteria thrive in high humidity and warm temperatures, and that is in part why NASA carefully controls these factors aboard the space station. In addition, spacecraft are not outfitted with carpets or attractive draperies, which would hold moisture in their fibers and therefore create a sweet hangout for microbes to grow. And while an astronaut's job comes with many perks of being a modern hero, even astronauts have to do their chores: space station crews have to do their "housework" just like everyone else, using disinfectants to keep the microbe balance in check. So the next time you're cleaning your bathroom, just think about how you have something in common with astronauts, and suddenly you will feel so much cooler about scrubbing your toilet! But what happens if astronauts slack off and skip their chores? Or the systems do not work as designed? Some serious ewww. (See the feature on page 118 for a real-life example . . . but be warned: you may not want to read it on a full stomach.)

The biggest problem with little microbes is that they are everywhere and in just about everything, including on and in human bodies. And everyone has different kinds and levels of them, depending not only on our genetic makeup but also on where we go, what we eat, and what we do. So imagine how difficult it must be for NASA to keep a close watch on the microbiology of every single person involved with the space station. Every astronaut involved in a space mission has been studied extensively to determine which microbes are hitching a ride. "There's no book or website that can tell you what's in urine or sweat," Román says, "because it's different for everybody at any given time. So we have to collect samples from the astronauts and do lots of hands-on studies and tests. When you exercise, you release different levels of ammonia and other chemicals, so NASA engineers designed a test facility on the ground where NASA test subjects exercise, and then we collect their sweat and see how the different chemicals in their sweat go up or down. It also depends on what they've eaten. It even depends on what chemicals you may have come into contact with the day before. Were you around pesticides? Or did you stop and put gas in your car?" And while you may think sampling sweat and urine is a dirty job, Román loves it because she gets to study all those microorganisms. "It's such a field day for me! It is like playing detective!" she exclaims.

Growing up in Puerto Rico, Román never dreamed that one

day she'd be having so much fun with astronaut pee! In fact, this was *so* not the future her parents saw for her.

[THE SPARK

Monsi grew up with little extended family. Both her parents were only children, so she and her three brothers and one sister had no aunts, uncles, or cousins. Because Monsi's dad was from Spain, she never got to see her grandparents there. "We were too poor to travel to visit them," she explains. Her grandmother on her mother's side, though she herself went to school only through sixth grade, valued education and made sure that Monsi's mother got a college degree in languages. Monsi's father did not attend college but made a living as a cash register mechanic. Román recalls her parents' aspirations for her and her siblings: "The line we heard over and over when we were growing up was 'Our daughters are going to be secretaries, and our boys are going to be engineers.' Even as a child, I thought that wasn't right." Luckily for young Monsi, her elementary school was part of a federally funded program to help encourage science education.

"When I was in fourth grade, we were told to go to the library and do research on something that interested us. I was so excited. I still have my proposal! I chose sharks. I grew up at the beach and loved fishing, and we had aquariums in our house. We'd pick up fish and put them in it. I loved watching them. We had an octopus and seahorses that we'd caught and brought home. So I did my study on sharks."

Román describes her young self as "smart

but restless," and surprisingly for a STEM leader, she disliked math. "I was a touchy-feely scientist very early on," she explains. "I wasn't the kind who could sit down. I'm good at memorizing and was always inquisitive. If the teachers taught me one fact, I had twenty follow-up questions. I would bug them to death! Some were OK with that and others didn't like it. But with math, they wanted to teach it in a way I couldn't understand. It was just a paper with problems on it. You could memorize it, but it meant nothing. They never showed us how to apply any of it. It was like, 'Here are flash cards. Memorize them.' I guess I learned something about math in high school because I took the AP math exam and did well enough to skip my first two years of college math. But I don't remember a single math teacher who made me want to do anything besides run away from school!"

But oh, the science fairs!

"I always won a medal," Román says. "In sixth grade, my dad helped me put together my project since he was good with building things. He built an aquarium for me to my specifications. One side had salt water and the other had fresh water. I wanted to see what would happen if I changed out the fish that lived in each type. Of course, I killed everything. There was always something crazy like that going on in my mind. I guess I must have explained it well, though, because I got a medal, just like I did on all my science fair projects."

As much as she disliked math, Monsi loved biology. "I had no idea what I wanted to do with it," she says. "I announced in sixth grade that I was going to study biology and people all said, 'Do you want to be a doctor?' and I said, 'No, I just want to study biology.' Culturally, at that time, girls were not supposed to like science that much, but some of the teachers still encouraged me. At some point, a magnet high school was founded nearby, and they sent the top hundred students there, and I was one of them. I loved it because at this magnet school, being a nerd was OK. And there was a fair amount of other girls there, too. I made close friends with another girl who was good with organizing and making things pretty. She and I found someone with the Environmental Protection Agency who got us clearance to study the levels of insecticides used on our island and how much of those insecticides got into the water supply and how they could harm the living organisms in the water. My friend and I ended up a great team because I was messy and unorganized, but I did good science, and she could make the pretty poster for it, and we wrote the essay together. We won first place." The prize included an invitation to the next level of the competition, to be held in the United States, but neither Monsi nor her friend could afford the trip. But that didn't stop Monsi from continuing to experiment.

"I loved studying animals," she recalls. "One time, I got lucky and found a bat in my front yard, so I took it to school and terrified everyone with it. I was so happy with my bat! At another point, I got some rabbits so that I could use them to perform some tests I'd read about. Back then they used rabbits to test cosmetics and lotions to see how their skin would react. But I couldn't bring myself to follow the protocols because I felt so sorry for the bunnies. So I wound up with some new pets instead."

Socially, Monsi had friends who have remained close to her even as an adult, but she describes her younger self as "very odd." She explains, "I grew up with a different culture than the other kids because my father was from Spain. The Puerto Rican kids didn't eat the Spanish food my family ate. My dad made me enunciate because in Spain, they really pronounce their words, but in Puerto Rico, they don't do that. So I talked 'funny' compared to my peers. And since I never had cousins to help socialize

me early on, I wasn't exactly a loner, but I wasn't a social butterfly, either. I was skinny and never thought I was very pretty, and I was not good at sports. And because we lived far from my school, I couldn't participate in after-school activities. Even if we'd lived closer, we couldn't have afforded things like that anyway."

While she liked her social studies classes, it was her science classes that made Monsi feel more accepted for who she was. "To see my third- and fifth-grade science teachers so in love with science helped me a lot," she says. "I remember them showing us, hands-on, what all the things in the book meant. They would do experiments in front of the class and get us all involved. And when I would bring projects in that weren't artsy and pretty, they made me feel proud and didn't treat me like an oddball. They said I had used good science, and they encouraged me."

Although her family struggled financially, Monsi was able to go to college on a scholarship, getting accepted to the university of her choice, where she would go on to graduate with honors. Early in her studies, she unexpectedly found her passion. "I signed up for a microbiology class because the other science classes were full, and this one had slots open because nobody else wanted to take it," she says. "The teacher spoke English, and that's another reason a lot of people didn't want to try it. He was a visiting professor from University of California, Berkeley, named Dr. Hazen. He was tough. He knew what we were capable of, and he expected it. He would fuss at us if we made bad grades, but I just fell in love with the class. Dr. Hazen let me work in his lab, and it changed my life. I realized that, in microbiology, you can do anything. I got to do fieldwork at the beach, and what could be better? And since I'd always been good at memorizing, I could easily remember the names of different diseases and what caused them. There was so much to study and learn! As I continued in the program, Dr. Hazen would take us to conferences with him in the United States and expect us to give presentations in English. We were terrified! He would introduce us to scientists whose work we had read about in the academic journals. We got to talk to them and see that they were real people, not just myths."

Monsi's family wasn't quite as excited as she was about her new sense of purpose. "My mom and grandmother wanted to know what I was going to do with a degree in microbiology," she says. "So I tried to think practically and even looked into becoming a dentist, but I hated it." During her first year of college, Monsi's parents divorced, making the family's financial situation even harder. "It was terrible," she recalls. "Some days, I would spend all day in school with one meal because I couldn't afford to eat. If Dr. Hazen hadn't started paying me as a research assistant, I don't know what would have happened. But the whole time, I always knew I would do what I was meant to do, so it never felt to me like I was fighting against something."

[THE EUREKA MOMENT

"Maybe it's a cultural thing, being from Puerto Rico, but I have never felt that anything I accomplished belongs exclusively to me," Román says. "I always feel like whatever we accomplish, it's as a team—especially at NASA. We are all about the team here." Román also explains that it's difficult to make one big discovery in the field of microbiology because there are so many variables. "You can never say $A + B = C$," she says. "That never happens. If you grow an organism, and you change one thing, it's hard to predict what the bacteria will do. They are so unpredictable. And like people, all bacteria are different. For example, you could study all the good microorganisms in your gut, and then if you got sick with a stomach flu or something and killed the good bacteria, and then you tried to re-create the exact same combination, you can't guarantee you'll get the same results." It's these sorts of variables that make working with microorganisms in spacecraft so difficult—and so hard to explain to others who work in more precise fields, where A plus B *does* always equal C.

"Back when I first started working on microbiology at NASA, the engineers wanted to understand biofilms," Román recalls. "I had to explain what that was and why they should be concerned about it, so we had to spend years studying biofilms and how to prevent them from getting out of hand. We did all kinds of system designs to see what would cause dirty water or a bad smell or whatever, but we could never re-create what we were trying to show them." As Román and her team learned, sometimes the best lessons are learned when things go really haywire.

"We had a urine processor to recycle urine on the space station," she remembers. "Someone had left fluids in it, and there was no flow through those lines for quite some time." As you'll recall, when liquid stops flowing, bacteria build up and clog the lines. "When they went back and turned on the machine, the hoses broke," says Román. "It was the biggest mess because the lines were so plugged up. I remember that day, laughing my head off, because I was like, 'Aha! I told you! This is what I've been trying to explain!' Of course, it generated a lot of extra work, cleaning up the mess and repairing the lines, but to me, it was totally worth it because everything we had predicted would happen actually did! I got to tell everyone on the team, 'See? Now you believe me! We have to be careful with our microorganisms!'"

That wasn't the only big lesson Román and her team learned from pee.

You already know that astronauts lose tremendous amounts of calcium while in space and that this is one factor that makes their bones more fragile (for a quick refresher on bone-density loss in astronauts, refer to our chapter on Dava Newman and the BioSuit). But how does that calcium actually leave their bodies? That's right . . . through their urine. No one realized just how big of an issue this was, though, until all that excess calcium affected the space station's plumbing.

"One of the biggest failures we had was with the calcium in the urine," Román explain. "It was hard on the pumps because calcium is very abrasive. So we had issues with that. But trial and error can be the best teacher in science. We all knew that astronauts lost a lot of calcium and how it exited their system, but the amount of calcium released by humans in the space station was much larger than what we thought we'd be dealing with." So Román and her team did what scientists always do when faced with a problem: more testing. "We had to test a lot of urine and run a lot of experiments on urine from the space station," she says. So when you fail at something, just think of it the way Román and other top scientists do . . . as a learning opportunity.

[NOTE TO SELF

Román would tell her younger self, "Follow your heart, and don't let anybody discourage you." When she was your age, she never thought she'd be working at NASA. "I don't even remember watching the moon landing when I was a kid, so NASA was never on my radar. But I met my husband in high school, and he was a math whiz," she says. "He became an engineer and got a job at NASA, and that's how I ended up in Huntsville, Alabama. Back when we came to the United States in 1985, there were only two jobs open at NASA that had anything to do with microbiology: one was working with engineers, and the other was in the lab. I got the first one. I felt so dumb, and I looked around and wondered how I was going to do it. I thought, 'These are NASA engineers, and here I am, designing a space station to keep astronauts alive, and if we make a mistake, they die.' But at NASA, we rely on teamwork and trusting one another and ourselves. That helped me to get over any anxiety and to feel like, 'OK, let's do this!' And it was so rewarding, and to this day, I really love what I do. Back then, I was the lowest-paid person in the group, but I took risks and kept myself humble, and now I'm one of the managers. I think that shows that if you love what you do, you'll be really good at it because you will always want to get better and learn more."

[NOTE TO YOU

Román's advice for you? "Find a mentor!" she urges. "Plenty of people will tell you that you're dumb or that your ideas are dumb, but there's at least one person out there who will tell you you're awesome, so find that person and tune out the others. Hang onto those people. Get that one yes and ignore the ten nos. Be grateful to those who help you, and when you get the chance, return the favor by mentoring someone else."

Finally, Román hopes you'll dig in your heels and keep going no matter what obstacles are in your way. "Don't give up," she says. "The hard stuff makes you stronger."

[WORDS TO LIVE BY

Román has three words to live by to be successful: "Take the risk."

"Always take the risk. Don't underestimate yourself," she says. "That's something I've learned over the years. If you're trying to decide if you want to do something, follow your heart and take a risk. You'll never have the perfect environment. I had such a small knowledge of microbiology when I started at NASA, compared to now. I started out in a job that was really high pressure because in that position, if you make a mistake, everybody's going to know. But if I'd run away in fear of that . . . well, I hate to even think about it!"

REMEMBER THE *MIR*: MICROBES' BIGGEST, GROSSEST SPACE PARTY EVER

WE TOLD YOU THAT if space station crewmembers aren't fastidious in their housekeeping, things can get really gross really fast. Russian astronauts found this out the hard way back in the early part of the twenty-first century.

It all started in 1986. The *Mir* space station was hailed as a marvel—a science lab in the sky! They did cool things like growing wheat from seed in outer space. The very name *Mir* translates into English as "peace." People who looked up at the night sky could see its lights among the stars and have hope for what humankind could accomplish.

And while *Mir* was amazing in many ways, this would-be triumph of the human spirit wound up becoming a giant, nasty mess.

Mir stayed up in space much longer than expected—fifteen years total. During those years, many different astronauts came to work on board the vessel, all bringing their own special bodily microbes along with them. And as those years passed, all those different microbes got to know one another while they were trapped together in a relatively small space . . . and the funk grew.

Astronauts eventually noticed, hey, something smells kinda weird here. And when they went to investigate . . . oh, boy! Behind panels on the space station, where the humidity and temperature—a balmy 82 degrees Fahrenheit (28 degrees Celsius)—made a perfect habitat for microbes, the astronauts found globs of brown and opaque-white water the size of *basketballs* (!!!) floating around in the zero gravity. Once astronauts got over the *blech* factor long enough to take samples of the globs, they found all kinds of things living in them. They found lots of different types of bacteria, fungi, protozoa, and even dust mites. And that was just the stuff behind the panels. It turns

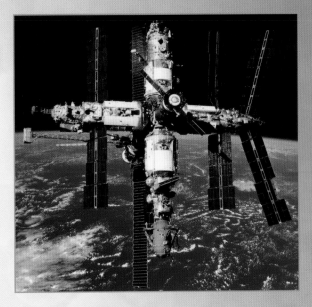

out that microorganisms had been growing elsewhere on the *Mir*, which explained a lot of system malfunctions and things breaking or clogging.

People feared that when *Mir* reentered Earth's atmosphere, we'd be overtaken by Nasty, Gnarly Monster Microbes from Outer Space, which would be a great title for a bad sci-fi movie, but nothing we'd personally want to experience. Luckily, the *Mir* deorbited without incident into the South Pacific Ocean, and Earthlings were not forced to bow down to evil bacterial overlords. But doesn't just the thought of it make you want to go clean something *right now*?

KAITLYN SADTLER

Engineering the Immune System for Tissue Regeneration

You probably already know that some animals have the amazingly awesome ability to regrow their bodily tissues, like how lizards can grow new tails or sharks can replace their teeth. You probably also know that we humans, unfortunately, can't do the same. Bummer!

But that's not entirely true. Your body does heal tissue all the time, which is why a cut or bruise on your skin usually heals itself without too much effort on your part (although the occasional adhesive bandage and some antibiotic ointment do come in handy). But severe burns and injuries aren't so easy to fix. Unlike salamanders, if we lose a leg, we can't just grow a new one . . . yet.

"Growing a new arm or leg is kind of our pie-in-the-sky dream," says immunoengineer Dr. Kaitlyn Sadtler. "It's not ruled out yet, but something like that would be many years in the future." It's a future, however, that Sadtler is working toward. And in the meantime, thanks to her and other researchers in her field, some pretty amazing things are happening in the study of tissue regeneration.

To help the body to grow new tissue, researchers first implant material as a scaffold (a structure to build upon). The first trick when implanting a scaffold is to keep your body's immune system from recognizing the scaffold as a hostile invader and going all out to destroy it. That's where Sadtler comes in.

"The same cells that fight off disease also help with tissue growth," Sadtler explains. Sadtler is researching ways to prevent what she calls the body's "splinter response": "If you get a splinter in your finger, your body is like, 'GET IT OUT GET IT OUT GET IT OUT!'" she says. "Same kind of thing if you've ever had your ears pierced. Your body is like, 'Hey, there's something here that's not supposed to be.' So you may have a reaction as your body tries to fight it, which we call the 'foreign-body response.'"

At this point you may be thinking, "Great! Let's just get rid of our immune systems, then, and all start regrowing limbs like superheroes!" Well, let's not get carried away. We're not knocking the human immune system. It is truly amazing. (To find out just how amazing, see the feature on page 131.) But if our immune system could chill out at certain times when we want it to, that would be great, too. Take, for example, allergies.

If you suffer from seasonal allergies, you may get a stuffy or runny nose and even, eventually, a full-blown sinus infection at certain times of the year. If someone asks what's making you sick, you might say, "The pollen makes my nose run." That's actually incorrect. It's not the pollen that's making your nose run; it's your immune system's *response* to the pollen. For whatever reason, your body thinks pollen is a dangerous enemy that must be defeated at all costs, so it's sending all those little soldiers to the battlefront (your nasal tissues) trying to keep the invaders out. The medicines you take are targeting your body's responses, trying to tell your body to take it easy. Sadtler's research is kind of similar in that she's looking for ways to tell the immune system to take it easy, or respond differently, to other things it might want to attack. She says, "In tissue regeneration, we want your body to work *with* the scaffold instead of fighting it. I work with a set of materials that work well with the body's immune response so it won't fight the scaffold."

Her research has also revealed that T cells—thymus gland cells that play a big role in the body's immune response—play particularly well with these new scaffolding materials.

So far, the work being done is on tissue that connects and strengthens parts of the body. For example, some breakthroughs have been made with regrowing tissue for diabetics who have ulcers that don't heal properly, or repairing hernias (weak spots in muscle or connective tissue). Some regenerative work has even helped injured military veterans regrow functioning muscle destroyed in small bomb blasts. In a few cases, functioning muscle has been regrown in limbs that would otherwise have required amputation! But we're still a long way from growing whole new limbs, because arms and legs contain more than just one type of tissue. For now, scientists such as Sadtler are excited to see success in regrowing tissues such as muscle and skin. However, the likely future of this type of biomedical engineering is astounding. If you want to see something that will blow your mind, stop here and do a quick internet search of "ghost heart." We'll wait.

Now that you're back, and as excited about the future of regenerative medicine as we are, you'll probably want to know more about how Sadtler became an immunoengineer. And you know we've got you covered!

[THE SPARK

Growing up in Frederick County, Maryland, in the 1990s, Kaitlyn was surrounded by "cows and cornfields," she says. "It was a lot more rural then; it's more developed now. But there were silos and cows down the street and cornfields behind my house. One girl on my bus would run through the cornfields to get home. It wasn't a big center for science and technology. Most people who lived there stayed there and there weren't a lot of new people coming in, but now it's become more urbanized."

Kaitlyn was the youngest of three children (she has a sister two years older and a brother twelve years older). Their dad, a Vietnam War veteran, worked in the telecommunications field for thirty-eight years after his time in the military. Kaitlyn's mother had grown up being told that the only acceptable jobs for women were in nursing or teaching. "She became a teacher," Kaitlyn explains, "but then she rebelled and went to work at a big tech company and did some early coding. But a background in hard science wasn't really in my family at all." Still, Kaitlyn's sister became a physical therapist, and because Kaitlyn enjoyed AP science and math classes in high school, she planned to become a doctor. Even so, Kaitlyn didn't count herself among her school's "smart kids."

"After kindergarten and before first grade, the school separated kids by ability, and they put me in the 'not-so-smart' class," Sadtler says. "My mom, having been a teacher, knew how important early development was, so she was like, 'Nope.' And she went to the school and had me moved because she didn't want me getting behind from the get-go. Later, we had a magnet program for gifted students, and I wasn't selected for that, either. But I did well throughout school and always had a strong work ethic. It wasn't until AP Calculus that I ever really outperformed other students in any way."

Sadtler credits much of her success in that course to her teacher Mr. Bolyard. "He was fantastic!" she says. "He was the high school teacher everyone wants to have. So fun! On Halloween, he always wore the dorkiest costumes. I remember one time, he wore a chicken hat and a blue sweater with a power cord draped across it and told everyone, 'I'm chicken-cord-on-blue!' He was also the first person with the school to tell me I could be something."

Socially, Kaitlyn was more of a "floater." As she recalls, "My high school had a very stereotypical, cliquish social system. You had the jocks, the anime kids, the Future Farmers of America, the brains, the popular girls, etc. I didn't fit with any of those groups." And while Kaitlyn had a core group of friends, she still experienced bullying. "I have no idea why I was targeted," she says. "I remember being on the playground in elementary school, and I was a quieter kid, but one day I became angry at how someone was treating me, so I said to her, 'We used to be friends!' and her response was, 'Yeah, and I used to be stupid, too!' Kids can be mean sometimes."

One thing that helped was sports. "I wasn't half bad at sports," she remembers. "But I was very sensitive to not getting picked for teams, and so I felt like, 'OK, I have been judged and found unworthy.' So I stopped thinking about sports in a hypercompetitive way. My dad was never one to push me too hard, but he supported my playing, so I found other outlets." Kaitlyn didn't make it onto her high school soccer team (which in hindsight was a bit

of a blessing—read on to find out how), so she decided to play with a county youth team that was glad to have her. "It was a men's club soccer team, and it was fun," she says. "All the guys on the team were really nice, and even though I was the only girl, they'd joke with me and have fun just like they did with everyone else. I was also captain of the swim team at my school, and that was a great group of students." Kaitlyn wouldn't discover her favorite sport, though, till college.

"I played rugby in college and it was fantastic!" she says. "I think all women should play rugby! It's such a rough sport, and you wind up having a great community because it's not hugely popular in the United States, so every time you run into someone who plays or has played, you immediately have something to talk about. Plus, it gave me such a feeling of strength and empowerment knowing that I was a woman who could go out and tackle someone and then give that person a hand up. No matter how physically aggressive the match, everyone is still friends at the end of it."

Kaitlyn decided to go to college at University of Maryland, Baltimore County (UMBC). She chose this school for a couple of reasons: first, she couldn't afford to pay the high tuition of some out-of-state schools, and second, her sister had studied biological sciences there and loved it. While studying at UMBC (which she also loved), Kaitlyn applied for a summer internship at the applied physics lab at prestigious Johns Hopkins University. As luck would have it, a friend from the men's youth soccer team she'd joined in high school worked there, and so did his dad. This connection helped Kaitlyn land the internship, and she did such a stellar job that the friend's dad, Charles Young, wound up becoming her mentor. In fact, Dr. Young told her, "I expect you to go to a top-ten graduate school." Inspired by his confidence in her,

Kaitlyn went on to get her PhD in cellular and molecular medicine at Johns Hopkins.

Sadtler now looks back on being cut from the girls' soccer team as a blessing in disguise. "If I'd made that team, who knows? It's possible that I might not have gotten that internship that shaped the rest of my career," she muses. We'd say that worked out well not only for Kaitlyn, but for the future of medicine, too!

[THE EUREKA MOMENT

Sometimes, simply coming from a different background than one's peers can make all the difference in big discoveries. "As far as the idea of research into tissue regeneration, the one different thing about me compared to most people in the field is that I worked in an immunology lab as opposed to a tissue-engineering lab," Sadtler explains. "I was jumping into engineering with my immunology background, which gave me a different approach. I had worked with T cells before I went to graduate school. So when I was doing my research, my thinking was, 'OK, what are these cells doing and why are they there?'" Could these T cells play a role in tissue regeneration?

This question kept nagging at Sadtler as she conducted her research, so she tried what might be called the Humpty Dumpty approach. "In biology, you break it, and then you see if you can put it back together again," Sadtler explains. "And that's what we did here. We did experiments where we took the T cells out and then we put them back in. Without the T cells, the regeneration would not work. But when we injected the specific T cells back in, the regeneration was rescued, and the immune signals once again began to correlate with improved tissue function. So basically, we broke Humpty Dumpty and put him back together again."

However, it took a fresh pair of eyes to see that ol' Humpty was, in fact, all fixed up. "I'd had a particularly exhausting series of consecutive sixteen-hour days in the lab, and after yet another day like that, I had a meeting scheduled with my thesis committee for later that afternoon. I was so tired that I just printed out my data and put it down in front of my committee chair. I kind of muttered, 'I think it worked,' and my chair took a look at the papers in front of him and was like, 'Yes, it definitely did! Don't you see? This proves our hypothesis!' I had been too exhausted to even recognize the impact of the data I'd put down on the table!"

The takeaway? Sometimes big ideas happen by chance, but most times, they happen as the result of good, old-fashioned hard work!

[NOTE TO SELF

"I guess if I could go back and give my younger self a message, I'd tell her it gets so much better," Sadtler says. "I wouldn't want to necessarily change anything because where I am now is the result of all the things that happened in my life."

Sadtler realizes now that even failures—maybe *especially* failures—have value. "Failures show you that you need to try something different, and the resilience that is born from them is so necessary. For those reasons, I wouldn't want to change too much because even the bullying I went through as a kid made me resilient," Sadtler says. "So I'd tell my younger self to be resilient, and stubborn, and imaginative, because you'll need those qualities in science. And I'd tell myself to stick with it and don't give up because middle school is hard for everyone."

. . .

[NOTE TO YOU

Like many of the other women in this book, Sadtler really hopes you're making the most of technology. "There are a lot of scientists out there, especially younger ones, who are really into outreach and connecting with people," she says. "They have all sorts of science festivals and summer programs, and with the internet, it's so easy to find them. I personally never went to science camp, but I would urge you to take advantage of social media and the net, because it's so easy to find these things now. A lot of them are free if you're limited by finances. I didn't know about a lot of things and didn't even think to apply for scholarships, but take advantage of the fact that you now have Google."

[WORDS TO LIVE BY

Because Sadtler's a self-professed "bit of a nerd," some of her favorite words of wisdom come from *Star Trek* character Jean-Luc Picard. Captain Picard tells an android struggling with indecision and insecurity, "It is possible to commit no mistakes and still lose. That is not a weakness. That is life." The general idea is that, even though you might fail, you must have the strength to try anyway.

"It may not be the most cheery motivational quote ever," Sadtler explains, "but it's definitely an important one because a lot of people don't talk about the failure that happens before you succeed." So don't let failures keep you down; success may be right around the corner.

MORE THAN A SNOT FACTORY: THE HUMAN IMMUNE SYSTEM

LET'S BE HONEST: the human immune system can be kind of revolting. When you get an infection, it produces nasty yellow pus (hard to believe it serves a purpose other than the gross-out factor, but it's actually full of neutrophils, which are white blood cells that fight infection). When you get a cold, it's responsible for the runny nose that just won't quit (if only science could figure out a way to make snot an alternative fuel, then we'd finally have a limitless supply of some truly "green" energy!). And when that simple cold turns into a full-blown sinus infection, complete with gunky, mucus slimeballs hanging out in your lungs, it's easy to forget that mucus is actually important for protecting the lining of your organs.

Go to any local drugstore and you'll find shelves stocked full of medicines that try to undo what your immune system does. You might start to think the immune system is just a giant pain in the neck (and it can be, when it causes your lymph nodes to swell).

But the fact is, the immune system is hardly the enemy. In fact, it's one of our greatest allies! Every minute of every day, your immune system is working hard to keep you alive. Unsung hero that it is, it has saved your life too many times to count, probably without your ever knowing it! And beyond saving us from infection, our immune cells are also huge players in wound healing and even maintaining neural connections in the brain. Yes, our poor immune system needs a good public relations campaign. To that end, here's an overview of the parts of your immune system, along with a brief description of each part's important job:

ORGANS OF THE IMMUNE SYSTEM

1. Tonsils and adenoids
2. Lymph nodes and lymphatic vessels
3. Thymus
4. Lymph nodes
5. Spleen
6. Appendix
7. Peyer's patches
8. Lymph nodes and lymphatic vessels
9. Bone marrow

Tonsils and adenoids: These guys trap germs that try to sneak in through your mouth and nose.

Lymph nodes: Think of these as filters. They keep the bad stuff out of your body while letting the good stuff flow through.

Lymphatic vessels: Sort of like your veins and capillaries, but these vessels transport lymph (a germ-fighting, white-blood-cell-rich fluid) throughout your body.

Thymus: Think of the thymus as the coach that trains your body's T cells to fight deadly germs.

Spleen: A true multitasker, the spleen not only recycles old red blood cells but also stores platelets and white blood cells.

Peyer's patches: You might call them the Gut Police. Found in your small intestine, they keep bad bacteria from taking over and protect good bacteria necessary for your digestive system.

Appendix: No joke: no one actually knows for sure what your appendix even does! Some think it has something to do with storing good bacteria for your intestines, but others believe it's about as important as whatever happens to be in the back of your kitchen's junk drawer.

Bone marrow: You know all those blood cells that fight infection? They're made in your bone marrow.

SARA SEAGER

Searching the Cosmos for Another Earth

[**FACT FILE**

HOMETOWN: Toronto, Canada

EDUCATION: BS in Mathematics and Physics, University of Toronto (1994); PhD in Astronomy, Harvard University (1999)

EMPLOYMENT: Class of 1941 Professor of Physics and Planetary Science, Massachusetts Institute of Technology

TOP HONORS AND ACHIEVEMENTS: Royal Astronomical Society of Canada Honorary Lifetime Member (2012); MacArthur Fellowship (commonly called a "Genius Grant") (2013); National Academy of Sciences Member (2015)

You've probably read a few books and seen at least a few movies about aliens. Many people consider aliens the stuff of science fiction, and those who talk about searching for them often aren't taken very seriously. But then again, most of those people aren't Dr. Sara Seager. Seager is not only a professor of astrophysics at MIT; she's also a world-renowned expert and foremost authority in her field. So yeah, people take her very seriously . . . and she is, in fact, searching for alien life.

Before you exclaim, "I knew it! That kid in my class is totally from another planet!," let's clarify a couple of things. First of all, Seager is looking for alien life on other planets (so give the kid in your class a break), and second of all, "alien life" doesn't necessarily mean "little green humanoids with ray guns" (although that might be kind of awesome if they were friendly, no?). Seager, when searching for alien life, would be perfectly pleased—even ecstatic—to discover a plant. Why?

Well, the presence of plants would tell us something extremely important about a planet—can you guess what it is? (Think about it, and we'll get back to that in a minute.) Also, plants are organic, meaning they are living things. And you know what living things need to survive? An environment that allows them to live. That sounds pretty easy, but it's really not.

You see, Earth is ridiculously special. It has all kinds of stuff that humans and other life require—including oxygen, water, and a temperature that doesn't burn us into ash.

So in order to find alien life, Seager is searching for a planet that has cool thanks-for-letting-us-live-here stuff like Earth has.

At this point you may be thinking, "Hey, there aren't that many planets, so why doesn't Seager just start by studying Mercury and eventually work her way out to Neptune?" But the fact is, those few planets you memorized in school are just the planets in *our* solar system (which is centered around just one of at least a hundred billion stars in our galaxy). There are literally billions of galaxies besides ours in space. And in those galaxies are billions and billions of stars that should each have at least one exoplanet orbiting them, just like the planets in our solar system orbit our star, the sun. (The word "exoplanet" is what they call a planet that orbits a star other than the sun.) So now you see why Seager won't be wrapping up this project anytime soon. She's begun a project to explore thousands of the nearest planets. How does she do it?

You may picture Seager sitting on a mountaintop on a clear, starry night, looking through a powerful telescope. While that's a beautiful image, it's far from reality. The fact is, Seager works mostly on her computer, just like the rest of us. And she's studied some pretty amazing exoplanets that way. (Check out page 144—especially if you're a *Star Wars* fan. Trust us!)

The reason Seager is studying all these exoplanets is that she's looking for what scientists call another "Goldilocks planet"—one that's not too hot, not too cold, but just right. Basically, another Earth!

Thanks to the Hubble telescope, a large and super-handy space telescope that was launched in 1990 to orbit Earth, scientists have been able to view the atmospheres of exoplanets. This is important because when we know what the atmosphere is made of, we can determine whether that planet could potentially support human life. So far, no planets have fit the bill. But that hasn't deterred Seager.

Twenty-something years ago, when Seager first began studying exoplanet atmospheres, everyone told her it was impossible. But it turns out everyone was wrong. Now studying exoplanet atmospheres is a whole scientific field unto itself.

A little while ago, we told you that Seager would be ecstatic to find a plant on one of these exoplanets. Have you guessed why she would get so excited over a plant? Because if you have plants, guess what else you have?

That's right: oxygen. Oxygen is one of the most important gases on Earth (we literally can't live without it, unless we give up breathing!), so in order to find another Earth, we first must

PHOTOSYNTHESIS

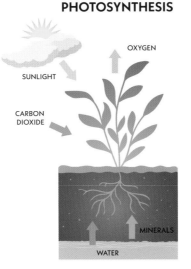

find oxygen in another planet's atmosphere. Seager believes not only that another Earth-like planet will actually be found, but that hundreds of years from now, our descendants will be traveling there.

But before we leap forward hundreds of years, let's travel backward to when Seager was just Sara, a girl growing up in Canada.

[THE SPARK

Sara's parents divorced when she was very young. She had a brother and also a sister, Julia, who was also her closest childhood friend. Sara recalls that she and her siblings were frequently left to their own devices. "Whether good or bad, my parents left us on our own much of the time," she says. "I would wander around the city of Toronto alone. I actually think it was helpful that they weren't always fixing things for me. I think I learned a lot for myself that way.

"My dad tried to expose me to art, music, and science," she says. "He took me to a 'star party' where volunteers had set up their telescopes. I was about five, and I loved it." Later on, a baby-sitter took Sara and her siblings camping, and Sara was thoroughly wowed by the night sky filled with stars. "My heart just stopped," she recalls.

You might expect us to say next that Sara made some amazing astronomy discovery when she was ten, but in fact, she tells us, "I wasn't the brainy kid in glasses doing experiments and blowing stuff up in the basement. I never even joined a science club or anything at that age." At sixteen, however, she fell in love with high school chemistry. "I couldn't believe you could explain the world around you with science," she says. "Things suddenly made sense and fit together so beautifully." However, Sara had trouble with the traditional take-notes-from-a-lecture learning environment. "School wasn't working for me because my learning style didn't allow me to process information the teacher was telling us or putting on the board," she says. "I couldn't focus, especially on hard concepts. I would go home and teach it to myself later. I was an active learner, so I'd draw diagrams and take notes on the texts I read. I was a pencil-and-paper person."

She recalls that one nontraditional class activity did click for her, though. Sara says her physics teacher used an interactive lesson to drive home the importance of mathematics: "The teacher held up a plywood board with a hole in it, and we had to get the right arc to get a spring to go through the hole from across the room by using formulas and the correct calculations of the angles. When my spring went through the hole based on the angle I had figured, I couldn't believe I could solve an equation to plan how something would happen in the world. It was amazing!"

Although she was a top student in her high school classes,

Sara often struggled socially because of an undiagnosed autism spectrum disorder, which caused her to be resistant to change and dislike things such as spontaneity and small talk. "I never fit in and was very awkward," she says. "When I was very little, I used to stare into space and cry a lot. My dad, being a doctor, had seen lots of babies and knew something wasn't quite right with me, but even physicians didn't know much about the autism spectrum back then. As I got older, I just didn't interact with other kids that much. I couldn't believe children played with one another; I didn't really understand how it worked. I was lucky that my sister Julia and I were only two years apart. She really saved me."

One benefit, however, of Sara's autism spectrum disorder was extreme focus. "That's one thing that helped diagnose me later in life," she explains. "I have always had unheard-of focus."

Probably a useful trait for someone undertaking the study of so many exoplanets, don't you think?

[THE EUREKA MOMENT

Because there are literally billions of exoplanets, how could Seager possibly prioritize which ones to study first when searching for an inhabitable planet? Wouldn't it just be like looking for a needle in a haystack . . . except that the haystack is space?

It occurred to Seager that Earth and Venus are called "sister planets" for a reason, which is that they have about the same size and mass. So why, she wondered, does Earth have tons of life while Venus has a massive greenhouse effect that makes it too hot to sustain life? The answer is in the planets' gases. "For nearly a century people have been thinking about gases in the planet atmospheres of other solar systems as life indicators," Seager explains. "The gases will tell you if a planet is inhabitable, so I knew that we had to study planets' atmospheres. Some planets will go in front of their stars, and that starlight enables us to pick up what is in the atmosphere. So I invented a big computer program to work out the concept of studying atmospheres this way."

While the right amount of starlight can be helpful to scientists like Seager, too much light can be, well, too much. For that reason, she and a team are developing a starshade that's basically a big screen that blocks out starlight so that a telescope can see the planet directly. The starshade looks like a giant flower attached to a telescope!

With innovations like this, it's exciting to think about how much more scientists might discover about exoplanets in the future. As Seager says, "For exoplanets, anything is possible under the laws of physics and chemistry."

An artistic rendering of the proposed starshade together with its telescope

[NOTE TO SELF

True to her extreme focus, Seager is succinct when asked what she'd say to her younger self. "I'd tell her it's OK not to have friends now because you will have friends later," she says.

[NOTE TO YOU

Seager has a few words of advice for you. First, she urges you to learn computer programming. "We're not ever going to get away from that," she promises. "Try to fit in an hour of coding every chance you get."

Second, when you're not coding, Seager urges you to take time off. "Kids today are so overscheduled," she laments. "They have no time to find out what they love doing. Finding what you love doing is really the key to success, but how do you find it if you don't have time?"

Third, embrace failure. "We really need to let kids fail," she says. "And if you don't win, you shouldn't get anything. Science is all about failing, and little failures prepare you for big failures. College students today can't seem to handle anything because they've never been allowed to experience defeat." So suck it up, buttercup . . . and give yourself a break! Failure just makes you stronger for the next go-round!

[WORDS TO LIVE BY

Seager has two aphorisms she really likes. The first is "Where there's a will, there's a way." The second is one she reminds herself of whenever she's trying to finish a project . . . even one as big as studying billions of exoplanets: "Keep your eyes on the prize."

"There may not be an actual prize," she says, "but still keep the finish line in mind."

A FEW OF OUR FAVORITE EXOPLANETS

SCIENTISTS HAVE DISCOVERED some amazing exoplanets! But would you want to visit them?

HD 40307 g: The name doesn't exactly roll off the tongue or scream to have its own travel brochure, which is why some have called it "Super Earth" (although it has yet to find a phone booth big enough for changing into its red cape). What makes it "super"? For starters, it's much more massive than Earth—about seven times more massive. This exoplanet's distance from its star is similar to the distance of Earth from our sun, so theoretically, it's the right distance to support life and potentially have water. And unlike many other exoplanets, it may rotate on its own axis fairly quickly, like Earth does, so that the same side isn't always facing the star, which means HD 40307 g may have day and night just like we do. The biggest issue scientists can see so far is that, in addition to being supersize, this "Super Earth" also has supergravity. Here on Earth, we have just enough gravity to keep us from floating away but not so much that we can't get around.

Kepler-1647 b: If you're a *Star Wars* fan, you'll be excited to know that some exoplanets orbit two stars, so if you were there, you'd see two sunsets just like Luke Skywalker does on Tatooine. The largest of these two-star planets (that we know of) is Kepler-1647 b, which is believed to be about the same age as Earth. However, its size is more like Jupiter, and so is its hydrogen composition, which means that it's unlikely to have living inhabitants. If the planet is also found to have a moon (or two, for that extra-cool factor!), however, then it's possible that water could exist on that moon, so the chance of a few Skywalkers watching that double sunset hasn't yet been ruled out.

Kepler-10b: Ever stood in a long line at an amusement park in August and felt like you were going to melt? Well, compared to Kepler-10b, your experience was like being dunked in ice water while eating a Popsicle during a snowstorm. Kepler-10b orbits much more closely to its star than Earth does to the sun (it's actually twenty times closer to its star than Mercury is to our sun), so if humans tried to visit there, we literally would melt (or turn into ashes . . . we're not sure which, so we're just going to stay here). So if you think 90 degrees Fahrenheit (32 degrees Celsius) is hot, try 2500 degrees Fahrenheit (1400 degrees Celsius) on Kepler-10b. That's hotter than flowing lava . . . so if alien life does exist there, they must have a never-ending and truly epic game of "The Floor Is Lava" going on.

BTW . . . Wondering why two of these planets are named Kepler? It's because they were discovered using NASA's Kepler space telescope. Thanks, NASA!

TERESA WOODRUFF

Safeguarding the Future of Girls with Cancer

[FACT FILE

HOMETOWN: Chicago, IL

EDUCATION: BS in Zoology and Chemistry, Olivet Nazarene University (1985); PhD in Biochemistry, Molecular Biology, and Cell Biology, Northwestern University (1989); Honorary *Scientiae Doctoris* (DSc), Bates College (2010); Honorary *Scientiae Doctoris* (DSc), University of Birmingham (2016)

EMPLOYMENT: Thomas J. Watkins Professor of Obstetrics and Gynecology, Feinberg School of Medicine, Northwestern University; Editor in Chief of *Endocrinology*, Journal of the Endocrine Society

TOP HONORS AND ACHIEVEMENTS: Presidential Award for Excellence in Science, Mathematics, and Engineering Mentoring from Barack Obama (2011); Guggenheim Fellow (2017); Elected to the National Academy of Medicine (2018)

How are babies made?" is a question you probably asked your parents at some point when you were younger. Dr. Teresa Woodruff of Northwestern University has been asking that question for the last few decades, but with a few added complexities.

Woodruff became famous in medical science in the early

twenty-first century when she created a brand-new branch of medicine dealing with reproduction . . . one that has the potential to improve the lives of girls following cancer treatment. Then, she made another important discovery about the fertilization process that may lead to greater success in the area of in vitro fertilization (reproduction begun in a lab instead of inside the human body).

Woodruff's first big contribution to medicine occurred in the early 2000s, when she was named director of the cancer center at Northwestern University's medical school. This was actually a bit unusual because Woodruff wasn't a cancer doctor. Those doctors are called oncologists, but Woodruff was a fertility specialist. However, because Woodruff had already been working at Northwestern, everyone knew how organized she was, so they asked her to oversee operations at the cancer center because they knew she'd make everything super efficient. While serving as director for the cancer center, Woodruff happened to notice a boy who'd come in to have his sperm put into storage. Cancer treatments, as you probably already know, are very tough on the human body: while killing cancer cells, radiation treatments and chemotherapy (cancer-fighting drugs) also kill healthy body cells such as hair cells and the reproductive cells of both boys and girls, sperm and eggs. Science had long ago figured out how to preserve boys' sperm by saving it in "banks" prior to cancer treatment so that when the boys grew up, they could withdraw their sperm and have a chance to have their own biological children. Banking sperm was standard practice. But when Woodruff saw this boy come into the clinic and was told what he was there for, she asked a very simple question: "What are we doing for the girls?"

The answer, sadly, was nothing. "We tell the girls not to worry about having children later in life, but just to concentrate on getting well," Woodruff was told. She found this unfair because she knew that boys and girls had the same cancer survival rates, so she asked, "Why are we worrying about boys' future fertility and not girls' future fertility?" Then she decided to do something about it.

And in true Wonder Woman style, Woodruff succeeded in making huge strides in tackling this problem! While scientists knew how to *remove* an ovary, they didn't know how to preserve it. So if someone wanted to save her ovary and fertilize an egg or two from it years later, she was out of luck. Woodruff figured out how to remove a single ovary from female cancer patients and isolate individual follicles that can be grown outside the body. Woodruff and other researchers are still working on the science involved (they have used this technology successfully to allow baby mice to be born, so they know something like this is possible), but one day, female cancer patients may be able to withdraw their saved ovaries from the bank when they want to get pregnant. Before Woodruff's work, nothing like this was ever dreamed possible! In fact, Woodruff literally created an entirely new branch of medicine that didn't exist before. Her field is called oncofertility because it combines cancer medicine (oncology) with reproductive medicine (fertility). New branches of medicine don't just happen every day, so it's safe to say Woodruff is kind of a big deal.

Oh, and by the way, while she was founding oncofertility, Woodruff made a huge discovery in reproductive health. She's responsible for finding what's known as the "zinc spark," a major discovery that can help infertile couples become pregnant. To review, the first step of pregnancy occurs when a (male) sperm joins with a (female) egg in a process called fertilization. Woodruff and her husband (more on that later!) co-discovered that when an egg is fertilized, a flash of zinc is released. The more zinc that is released from the egg, the more likely an embryo will be healthy. (Many more things contribute to overall embryo health, but this is the first and best marker of egg health that can be determined outside the cell.) The zinc spark could make a big difference to people relying on in vitro fertilization to have children. Why? Because the size of the zinc spark could allow doctors to predict which fertilized eggs will develop into healthy babies, which helps would-be parents have better chances of success. Before Woodruff's work, no one knew the zinc spark existed, so they weren't looking for it.

Wow! Creating an entirely new branch of medicine and discovering the zinc spark? Not too shabby! But before Woodruff became a pioneer in medicine, she was simply Teresa, a girl growing up in Illinois.

[THE SPARK

Teresa Woodruff grew up just south of Chicago. Her mom was a first-grade teacher, just like Teresa's grandmother, who'd taught in a one-room schoolhouse in Oklahoma during the Dust Bowl era (a seriously tough time in American history totally worth looking up online or in a library). Teresa's dad was a professor of theology (the study of God and religious beliefs) and biblical literature at Olivet Nazarene University. "My dad was from Kansas and went to college on the GI Bill after having fought in the Korean War," Teresa explains. "The government would pay for returning soldiers to go to college, so my dad took them up on the offer." Teresa's entire family valued education. "My parents and grandparents were all lifelong learners and great readers of books. They taught my two younger brothers and me to be curious about the world around us. Every summer, we went to different states and explored the natural world." Both parents nurtured her intellectual curiosity, and her grandmother influenced her ability to create new organizations that bring people together. "My grandmother was always starting groups to explore things," she recalls. "She started a music lovers' club, a bird lovers' club, and lots of artistic clubs in her community in Oklahoma. She created programs to help people around her. That was just her way of being. She was a self-made woman, and she just got things done, even during the Dust Bowl years when other families were giving up their farms. She stayed and has what is called 'true grit.'"

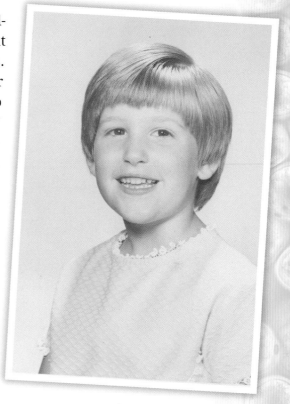

When Teresa was growing up, her mother taught summer classes for young children. Part of the curriculum involved math and science: "She would make volcanoes for them to study, and these little kids were actually using the word 'volcanology.' It was incredible!" Still, at that time, Teresa never thought she would pursue a career in STEM. "I wanted to be a first-grade teacher like my mom and grandmother," she says. "Mom always said that first grade is the most transformational time in anyone's life because you learn so many things, including how to engage complex ideas. I thought that was very exciting."

As a child and a teen, Teresa was extremely organized. "I was always trying to do things faster and ahead of time and come up with bigger and better projects," she says. She excelled in her school's gifted program and credits a class project on advertising with helping her learn how to organize people around ideas and work toward a common goal: "We had to create ads to sell a car or toothpaste. That was very enlightening to me in learning about networking and leadership."

Socially, Teresa says, she was "in between" with her peers. "I guess I was the 'brain' of my class, but I don't think I was a nerd. I got the highest award for a graduating female, but I also played softball and volleyball during high school, and I was in the orchestra. That was what I was most into. I'd started playing cello when I was about six or seven, and I continued that long into graduate school. There was this band when I was growing up called ELO, Electric Light Orchestra, that was really popular, and I dreamed of being in it! I had a white cello that I spun around in a very rock-star fashion!"

Teresa's favorite teacher was Mrs. Allen, who taught her in third grade. "She really challenged us and personalized our education," Woodruff explains. "I still see her frequently." Teresa also adored Mr. Cruz, her chemistry teacher, who taught her to love chemistry. In college, her favorite teacher was her father. "I went to college where he was a professor, and I got to take one of his religion classes. He made the material come alive with stories and multiple ways of teaching," she says. Other mentors included her orchestra teacher and her college biochemistry and physical chemistry professors.

Teresa studied elementary education in college, but because she was such an advanced student, she finished early. "My parents wanted me to be in college the full four years so I could enjoy developing as an individual before I went into the working world," Woodruff says. "They told me to pick something else to study after I had finished my education course load. I chose chemistry just because it was something I enjoyed. I didn't know anything about research or all the STEM fields that are available. All I knew was that people who liked chemistry became medical doctors, and the only kind of doctors I really knew of were pediatricians, so I started on that path." During her undergraduate studies, Teresa was invited to the California Institute of Technology to study how to turn toxins into vaccines. "After that," she says, "I was completely taken by the notion of science. I loved putting on that white lab coat! Something about putting on a lab coat and gloves makes you stand up a little straighter and really take seriously what you're doing."

[THE EUREKA MOMENT

When Woodruff asked that simple question at the cancer clinic, "What are we doing to preserve the fertility of girls with cancer?," it was life-changing for her and—someday, we hope—for girls with cancer. When the answer "nothing" wasn't good enough for Woodruff, she began years of work to come up with a better answer. "It turns out I was at the right place at the right time," she says. "You always want to bring a solution to a set of problems."

Speaking of the value of timing, Woodruff's discovery of the zinc spark had a lot to do with timing as well. In fact, the whole thing happened somewhat by chance. "My husband is a chemist who studies zinc, copper, and iron," Woodruff explains. "We take a walk along Lake Michigan every day, and one day during our walk, he told me he'd read something about zinc and sperm and asked me, 'Why is there so much zinc in human sperm?' and I responded with three of the most unfortunate words I've ever said in my life: 'I don't care.' You see, I'd devoted my career to studying the female egg, not sperm, so I wasn't interested in what sperm contained. And there was no evidence of zinc in the egg, and therefore no reason to look for zinc there; no scientist had ever devoted any time and attention to that. But since my husband had the tools to measure zinc, we thought we'd look into it because I told him if there's anything important for fertilization, it will be in the egg. And so we used his tools to check it out. So we're a little like Pierre and Marie Curie! We found that before fertilization, the egg takes up a lot of zinc, and that zinc is required for the egg to mature. At the moment of fertilization, the zinc is released from the egg in a spark.

"What's remarkable about how this came about is that most of science builds on some knowledge that went before, but this was a true discovery. There was no reason to go looking where we did, and it would not have worked except that an inorganic chemist who studies zinc and had all the tools was walking on the beach with his wife, who studies eggs! So this biological event was discovered just because of a random question during our daily walk. Most discoveries like this build on lots of previous research, but this discovery was truly serendipitous."

■ ■ ■

[NOTE TO SELF

"If I could talk to my younger self, I'd tell her this: Don't worry about the long game," Woodruff says. "Just think about the next step right in front of you. You don't have to think that far in advance. Just make individual steps that make sense for you at the time, and eventually, you'll look over your shoulder and find that you've walked a long distance."

[NOTE TO YOU

So many opportunities abound for kids today interested in STEM. Woodruff urges you to "look for opportunities in labs"—ask if you can observe or help out in the laboratory in some way. And take advantage of the ease of modern communication. "Don't be afraid to email folks like me to ask for a day during which you can shadow a student/scientist," Woodruff says. "There are lots of folks who want to help you achieve your goals!" Remember that many STEM geniuses, like Woodruff, are also educators, so they have a passion for bringing along the next generation in the field.

[WORDS TO LIVE BY

"My motto is 'Seek joy, avoid despair, never mock, never betray, smile, never point,'" Woodruff says. The last one, "never point," means not to blame others. "People externalize things and think it's always someone else's fault," she explains. "Don't blame other people when things go wrong. Just get to work on fixing the problem."

FIGHTING FOR FERTILITY IN KIDS WITH CANCER

WHEN CHILDREN ARE DIAGNOSED with cancer, the main focus is, of course, survival. The good news is that more and more children with cancer are surviving this dreaded disease. But as survival rates increase, the question of future fertility has become increasingly important. A lot of what can be done depends on how old the child is and whether the patient is male or female.

Inside a woman's ovary—and this may blow your mind—are approximately *one million* tiny little follicles, which are units that make hormones. Each of those roughly one million follicles contains a single egg that could be released for possible fertilization, and healthy fertilized eggs grow into babies. Of course, most of those eggs don't get fertilized (can you imagine having 999,999 brothers and sisters?).

Older girls with cancer have the option of freezing their eggs for later fertilization and implantation into the uterus. This technology has been around for a while, and while it's still not perfect (eggs have a lot of water inside them, and freezing them can cause ice crystals to form, which can damage the egg), doctors are working on it.

However, until puberty occurs, female bodies do not produce mature eggs. So for younger girls, the challenge was to protect their follicles from being destroyed by cancer treatments so that even girls whose bodies hadn't yet produced eggs would have the option of getting pregnant in the future if they wanted to.

That's why Woodruff's research into growing follicles outside the ovary is so groundbreaking . . . because it can potentially keep the possibility of restoring fertility sometime in the future.

Similar to girls, boys who have not yet undergone puberty also do not produce their reproductive component, sperm. In the case of young boys with cancer, doctors are investigating saving tissue from boys' reproductive organs and cryogenically freezing this tissue, then implanting it back into the patient once his cancer has been cured so that the undamaged tissue will allow his body to produce sperm normally. No one knows yet if sperm can be created from this testicular tissue, but for now, doctors are banking it in hopes that one day the technology will catch up. Doctors extract this tissue before the boy begins cancer treatment so that chemotherapy drugs and radiation therapy will not damage the tissue to be banked. The risk of re-implanting untreated tissue, though, is that it may still contain cancer cells and reintroduce those back into the body.

As you can see, the field of oncofertility has a lot of work to do. But this is still great news because generations ago, children with cancer had little hope of survival. The fact that oncofertility exists as a medical discipline is a testament to how far medical science has come and to the hope that cancer patients now have for a bright future.

MINJUAN ZHANG

Driving Automobile Technology to (Literally) Unseen Destinations

[FACT FILE

HOMETOWN: Longyou, Zhejiang, China

EDUCATION: BS in Materials Science and Engineering, Beihang University (1989); MS in Electrical Engineering, Shanghai Institute of Metallurgy, Chinese Academy of Sciences (1992); PhD in Electrical Engineering, Tokyo Institute of Technology (1997)

EMPLOYMENT: General Manager, Toyota Research Institute of North America

TOP HONORS AND ACHIEVEMENTS: *Design News*'s 15 Engineers Who Are Transforming the Auto Industry (2017); *Interesting Engineering*'s 15 Engineers Building the Tech of the Future (2018); R&D 100 Award (2018)

If you're like most kids, at some point you have probably played with Matchbox or Hot Wheels cars. Maybe you even had a favorite: a prized one with a sleek design and, of course, the most amazing color. Ah, the colors! Toy cars come in an amazing array of them! Real cars . . . not so much. Ever wondered why real automobiles come in a relatively small range of color choices

A Lexus LC 500 convertible in Structural Blue

as compared to their mini toy counterparts? Dr. Minjuan Zhang knows why. And it bugged her.

The reason real cars have limited color choices is because they're much larger (obvs!), and they have to withstand a lot more exposure to the elements than toy cars do. Sure, maybe you left your Hot Wheels out in the sandbox for a few days before your mom retrieved it, but with real cars, we're talking years of exposure to intense sunlight, rain, snow, hail, and wind. Automobile manufacturers have to take these factors into account when mixing paints to withstand the elements, and not every color can take the heat (or cold, as the case may be).

But in 2017, Lexus (a luxury division of Toyota) introduced a revolutionary color in its LC 500 series. This color, known rather modestly as Structural Blue, was the result of intense research on the part of Toyota's Minjuan Zhang, an engineer and materials scientist. Zhang took inspiration from morpho butterflies and studied how light interacts with their wings. Morpho butterflies actually have no pigments, but the structure of scales covering their wings causes them to appear a vibrant, iridescent blue when light hits them (learn more about this phenomenon in the feature on page 170). Zhang adapted this natural phenomenon in her work to make the Lexus LC 500 appear to be different shades of blue depending on how the light bounces off the car.

No kidding . . . it's a pretty sweet-looking ride. Fit for a superhero, in fact: you may have noticed that Black Panther himself drives one in the incredibly successful 2018 film!

The secret to how we see color is based in light refraction, meaning how the light is absorbed by or reflected by an object. You can play around with this yourself if you have some different-colored light bulbs. Light comes in different frequencies (see graphic below), and the color we see is the product of which of these frequencies the object absorbs. If your shirt appears white, it's because it's reflecting all the frequencies instead of absorbing any of them. But if you're wearing a blue or green shirt, that means that your shirt is absorbing only red frequencies and reflecting back green or blue.

VISIBLE LIGHT REGION OF THE ELECTROMAGNETIC SPECTRUM

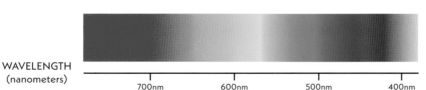

ENERGY INCREASES

WAVELENGTH
(nanometers)

700nm   600nm   500nm   400nm

The fact that Zhang was able to apply this science to create Structural Blue and create a paint formula that would survive an automobile's weathering is pretty amazing. The technology is so advanced that Zhang and her team won a 2018 R&D 100 Award, which is basically like an Oscar but for inventors—it's one of the most prestigious awards in the whole world for science and technology innovations. But was she done? Nope. Not even close. You're not even going to believe what she's working on next. Are you sitting down?

Zhang and her team at Toyota are currently working on making cars INVISIBLE. We know—your mind is blown! Ours are, too! The next thing you're probably wondering about is how a bunch of invisible cars won't constantly crash into one another . . . or how we'll ever be able to find the cup holders. Both are good questions! But don't worry; she's got it covered. The idea is not to make cars fully invisible (because, hey, that does sound like a traffic nightmare) but to make portions of the interiors invisible to the drivers so that they can better see the road. We'd love to tell you more about what Toyota plans to do with this amazing technology, but since these plans are so top secret (and rightly so), we couldn't really ask too many questions about them. For now, just know that Zhang is working on invisibility in automobiles, and let's focus on how she got to this point.

[THE SPARK

Minjuan was one of three children born to her parents in a small town in southeastern China. In the 1970s and '80s, when Minjuan was growing up, becoming a scientist was all the rage. "I chose to be a scientist because science was considered very cool," she says. "China promoted science as being important to our country's future. I wanted to be part of that." She recalls a biology assignment on butterflies that had a lasting impact, though she had no idea of its importance at the time. "After we learned about the butterfly's life cycle, my biology teacher taught me more about butterflies. I guess the beautiful butterfly colors really attracted me, and that's why I wanted to re-create their brilliant color in my later career." Zhang also remembers enjoying an assignment in physical science in which the teacher taught the class to use a ruler and a protractor to locate the position of the stars. "What an amazing thought, to use such simple tools to guide us to study the galaxy!" she says. But although these teachers helped further Minjuan's interest in science, she already felt destined for a future in STEM.

You see, Minjuan's mother had attended engineering school but had quit during her junior year when her own mother became sick and needed full-time care. Minjuan's mother later married and never returned to school. "I wanted to continue her dream by going to engineering school myself," Zhang explains. "My grandparents had always talked about how boys had the advantage because they could focus on their careers, while girls had to take care of their families when they grew up. But for me, I never felt that I was at a disadvantage to the boys. I was always the top student in my class. I would finish assignments faster than everyone else and get a perfect

score, too. And everyone in the class knew it. School in China was different than it is here. There was no confidentiality. In every class, the teacher would post academic scores next to our names, with the highest-achieving student at the top and the lowest-achieving student at the bottom. The person at the top naturally had a high social status. Because I was always at the top, other students would come to me for help, and I was always willing to help them. So I was sort of popular because the other kids came to me for their academic needs. But it also didn't hurt that we were one of the few families in town that had a television, so my friends would always come over after school for entertainment!"

The teachers at Minjuan's middle and high schools were usually young graduates who became mentors and friends. "They all liked me and became my friends. Some of them gave me nice books and told me about their college life and treated me special, as if I were more of a friend than a student," she says.

Although she enjoyed art class and painting as well as philosophy classes, there was little question what Minjuan would study in college. "China has changed some since then, but at the time, the idea was that smart people went into science and engineering," she explains. "And if you did well, you were likely to get the chance to study abroad for your PhD, which I really wanted to do because of my philosophy teacher. You might expect that a math teacher would have been my biggest inspiration, but in fact, it was this history and philosophy teacher who made a huge impact in my life. He really influenced me about Western culture and inspired me to want to go abroad. It was difficult to get offers from foreign countries to come study, but if you did well, that was an option."

Not surprisingly, Minjuan excelled in college during the late 1980s, even though there were only five girls and thirty boys in her class. This was a turbulent time in Chinese history: Chinese college students led demonstrations in Beijing demanding freedom and democracy. The Chinese government responded with military force in what is now known as the Tiananmen Square massacre. Zhang recalls that dark time in her home country's history: "I felt hopeless. All of us college students, including my husband [another student at her college], were protesting. It was terrible. In a stroke of fate, my husband and I were not in Tiananmen Square the day the military responded because we had gone to be with my family after my grandmother suddenly passed away from a heart attack." The government punished the organizers of the protest after the massacre, and the episode made Minjuan more determined than ever to study abroad. "After graduation, I wanted to go to a Western country," she says.

When she received an offer to study in Japan for her PhD, she quickly accepted. During the second year of her PhD program, Minjuan and her husband learned that they were expecting a baby. This was one of the biggest challenges of Minjuan's life. Minjuan wanted to take a break from school to take care of her child, but her mother urged her to reconsider. "It was a tough situation," recalls Zhang. "I wanted to take a year off, until my son got bigger. My dad was fine with that, but my mom insisted that I not do it, so I took only one month off from school when he was born. My mother didn't want me to take even a semester off because she didn't want what had happened to her to happen to me." Minjuan managed to take care of her child (with strong support from her mother) without compromising her chances of graduating. In fact, she still managed to get high marks. After her PhD work was completed, Minjuan worked in Japan for four years. When the family moved to the United States after her husband took a job there in 2001, Zhang took two years off and stayed home with her son, something she truly enjoyed. "But this time both of my parents pushed back," Zhang recalls. "My parents always reminded me that I did not have to be a housewife as was the case in the China of my grandparents. They wanted me to be an example of a modern woman who did not have to choose between a career and a family. That was exactly what I wanted since I was a child."

Zhang, who by this time had a bachelor's degree in materials science and engineering and a doctorate in engineering, found a position at Toyota in 2003 and began her career in the US. She is now considered one of the leading experts in nanomaterials (really, really small materials) and thin-film technology (coating objects in those really, really small materials). Looking back, Zhang is thankful for her parents' input. "Their thinking made me strong and tough. I'm glad now that I did what they wanted. I have two sons now, and they are both proud of me and the work I'm doing. Now that they're older, I've asked them if I should've stayed home with them instead of going back to work, but they tell me they are glad to have me as a professional role model, so that is my reward. That's what makes me feel that I did the right thing."

[THE EUREKA MOMENT

After joining Toyota, Zhang was given one specific assignment: color. "We see so many colors, but the colors available for cars are very limited because the paint has to be durable," she explains. "Cars are exposed to sun and rain and hot and cold and all sorts of weather over a long period of time, so it's not enough just to create a new paint color—that paint color has to last through all the exposure to the elements that the car will have." Zhang started thinking back to her days in school when she studied butterflies, particularly that beautiful blue one. "The color was so brilliant and rich," she says. "I started thinking about how we could make the same color on a car." Some of her colleagues thought it couldn't be done because the butterfly's color shifts with the viewing angle, but Zhang and her team began with a very small batch of Structural Blue and tested it over and over until they managed to keep the same color over an entire car. Toyota sent Zhang back to Japan for a full year to work with color designers to make Structural Blue more attractive and to work with other engineers on the paint's durability. "It was tough to solve the problem of making the paint hold up against the elements, but we did it. We worked with scientists and engineers with different specialties and passed all the tests." she said. In all, Structural Blue was fifteen years in the making, but it made quite a splash.

All this work to get a butterfly-blue car led to another idea. "We had to do a lot of work with light manipulation," Zhang explains. "We worked with so many different chemists and engineers with different specialties, and we did underwater tests and all kinds of simulations. Working with light simulations, we did experiments about how to bend light. That got me thinking about what other possibilities we could explore by bending light." And that's how the idea for invisibility came about. Toyota has filed a patent for a "cloaking device" on its vehicles that would be placed on the sides of a car's windshield. Mirrors would then be used to bend light, allowing drivers increased visibility. We don't know how soon Toyota might roll out this new (and super-awesome) technology, but if it becomes available, it could prevent crashes caused by limited visibility.

[NOTE TO SELF

Looking back, Zhang recalls that when she was a child, she felt like she could do anything. She feels that this belief may have actually hindered her. "If I could talk to my younger self, I'd probably tell her to focus on one area and start pursuing it early," she explains. "I'd tell myself to find a role model or seek out specific people in your area of interest so you can go deeper in your studies. You'll achieve more that way. I figured that out eventually, but it took me some time. I think as a young girl, sometimes I was a little too confident, thinking that I could be anything. I'd tell young me to focus."

[NOTE TO YOU

Got something you're curious about and want to explore? Zhang says go for it! "Today's teachers do such a great job with science classes," she says. "They take the kids on lots of field trips and help them understand the stuff behind the science. That helps them get motivated and spurs their creativity to develop and invent." Zhang loves watching her younger son, who was eleven years old at the time of our interview, work through solutions for everyday problems. "I guide him in his process, but he has these big ideas," she says. "One day, it was raining, and he said the windshield wipers were annoying and that we should come up with something else. I loved that he was thinking of solutions to problems. I taught him about benchmarking, which is comparing your method to the best thing going at the time and seeing how you can improve things. Now he goes through the benchmarking process when he comes up with ideas and questions. So I would tell all young people to identify something that interests you and dive in."

[WORDS TO LIVE BY

Zhang likes this quotation from business visionary Joel Barker: "Vision without action is merely a dream. Action without vision just passes the time. Vision with action can change the world." She explains, "This wisdom has really guided me to not just have a dream, but to realize that dream through my actions. You can always dream, but implement the idea. Stop talking about it and do it. It's important to dream, but it's even more important to make that dream happen."

WHAT MAKES THESE BUTTERFLIES SO BLUE?

AS YOU MAY ALREADY KNOW, butterfly wings aren't completely flat, but made up of many rows of itty-bitty scales. In most butterfly varieties, the scales are individually pigmented with different colors that, when viewed together on the whole wing, create patterns. For example, the monarch butterfly has that distinctive orange and black stained glass look, with polka dots around the edges. Each monarch scale has an actual color assigned to it. But blue is one of the rarest pigments in living things, and most animals cannot produce that pigment. The morpho butterfly gets its blue color by using what's called "structural color." This means that rather than having individual pigments on the individual scales, the scales instead bend and reflect the light that hits them.

Remember blowing bubbles as a small child? (Or maybe even yesterday? No judgment here . . . bubbles are cool!) What made them so magical? Sure, they floated around on the breeze and then disappeared in a single pop, which is probably some life lesson if you want to get all philosophical, but another magical aspect of bubbles is their iridescent rainbow color. In truth, the bubbles themselves have no color. Those groovy pinkish/bluish/orangish waves you see are the result of *interference*. Interference occurs when two light waves coincide and form a new light wave.

CONSTRUCTIVE INTERFERENCE

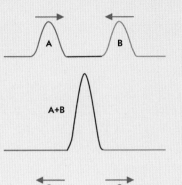

BEFORE
INTERFERENCE

DURING
INTERFERENCE

AFTER
INTERFERENCE

DESTRUCTIVE INTERFERENCE

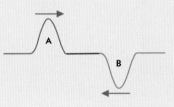

BEFORE
INTERFERENCE

DURING
INTERFERENCE

AFTER
INTERFERENCE

As we explained earlier in this chapter, white light is made up of many different wavelengths, each corresponding to a different color. The rays of white light hitting the back of the bubble's thin film "interfere" with the light rays hitting the front of the film, and depending on the angle of the light and the thickness of the film, some of the wavelengths experience constructive interference and are enhanced, and some experience destructive interference and are suppressed. That's why we see the colors we do.

Another way structural color works is through *diffraction*. You know that sort of rainbow you see on CDs? It's caused when the CDs' regularly spaced grooves spread out the rays of light that hit them.

INCIDENT
WHITE LIGHT

Morpho butterfly wings use both interference and diffraction to play with the light and produce the blue we see, and that blue looks different depending on the angle you're viewing it from.

While Zhang and her team at Toyota developed complex processes to create layers of pigments and metals that would mimic the way the morpho butterfly's scales reflect light, morphos somehow manage to do it all naturally. It's such a complex process that biologists are still trying to figure out how they develop these incredible light-bending scales. If you happen to run across a talking morpho butterfly, be sure to ask how they do it and get back to us ASAP!

ACKNOWLEDGMENTS

Many thanks to the twelve scientists profiled in this book, who were incredibly generous in granting us interviews, answering our questions, and reviewing our work. Any errors that remain are our own. Thank you also to Andrew Dennis, Jack Little, Kim Ouderkirk, Grace Siy, Harold Stowell, Brian Walker, and Christine Jeana Yates for providing additional scientific expertise. Thank you, too, to Abigail Samoun for finding the perfect home for this project.

GLOSSARY

BASIC: Beginner's All-purpose Symbolic Instruction Code; a programming language first developed in the 1960s

benchmarking: the practice of comparing a new product or technique to the best previously developed version

biofilm: an accumulation of microorganisms on a surface

biomechanics: the study of the structure and motion of living things

bioprinting: a technique for creating 3-D shapes out of living cells

bone density: a measure of the amount of bone mineral in a bone; lower numbers are associated with a higher risk of breakage

celerity: speed

diffraction: a change in the direction of waves as they encounter an obstacle

disarmament: reducing or eliminating weapons

DOS: disk operating system; computer software that allows a computer to perform basic functions

ecology: the study of the relationship between organisms and their environment

electrodes: small pieces of metal that transmit an electric current

exoplanets: planets outside our solar system

extrapolation: extending known data to predict unknown data

fission: the act of splitting something apart

follicle: a group of cells surrounding a hole in which something grows

frequency: the number of waves that pass a point in a given amount of time

fusion: the act of joining things together

gamma ray: a high-frequency form of radiation

immune system: a system of cells and organs that protect the body from foreign invaders

in vitro fertilization: reproduction begun in a lab instead of inside the human body

interference: the process in which two waves superpose to create a resultant wave

iridescence: the phenomenon of an object appearing to change color when you look at it from different angles

isotope: a version of a chemical element

mass: the amount of matter ("stuff") in an object; a constant measurement regardless of the amount of gravity

microbes: microscopic organisms

microgravity: very weak gravity

MRI: magnetic resonance imaging; an examination that allows doctors to see inside a body

neutrons: subatomic particles with no electric charge

noncompliance: failure to act in a prescribed way

nonproliferation: a slowing down or stopping of the spread of something (especially nuclear weapons)

qualitative data: non-numerical data

quantitative data: numerical data

radiation: the emission of energy in the form of waves or particles

radioisotope: a radioactive isotope

refraction: a change in the direction of waves as they pass from one medium to another

regeneration: the formation of new tissue

representative sample: a small part of a group that reflects the same characteristics as the whole group

scaffold: a structure to build upon

sediment cores: long cylindrical samples of Earth's crust layers that can be analyzed to reveal changes in the environment over time

statistics: the study of large amounts of data

stem cells: cells that have the potential to turn into different kinds of cells, depending on what the body needs

sustainable development: economic activity that does not deplete natural resources

T cells: cells that play a critical role in the immune system; called T cells because they develop in the thymus

SUGGESTIONS FOR FURTHER STEM AWESOMENESS

Now that you're thoroughly inspired by these amazing Wonder Women of STEM, why don't you go ahead and be STEM-wonderful yourself? Here are some things you can do right now!

1. Find a summer program in a field that interests you. Colleges and universities all over the country offer intensives for young students in a wide range of subjects. You might go to engineering camp, for example, and get a head start on deciding which field of engineering is for you . . . or you might find that engineering isn't your thing after all. Either way, you'll be a step closer to finding your STEM passion. Camp options are almost endless, so find something you love and dive in! (FWIW, Tiera has a special place in her heart for NASA's Space Camp!)

2. Seek out a mentor. Know of someone who's doing exactly what you want to do when you grow up? Reach out to that person and tell them so! They'll probably be thrilled to hear from you and may offer priceless advice. They might even let you shadow them at work so you can see exactly what a day-in-the-life entails.

3. Pay it forward. Are you great with numbers? A whiz with science? Offer your services at a kids' program or as a peer tutor to someone who's struggling.

4. Join the club. Whatever your interest, there's probably a club for it. Many student and professional organizations exist just for members with similar ethnic or regional backgrounds. Search online and find your people!

5. Try something outside your comfort zone. Maybe you love chemistry but not so much biology, or you enjoy building things but not so much writing about how they're built. Stretch yourself and try something you've never tried before. You might find that you like it a lot more than you expected.

6. Nurture your non-STEM side. STEM makes the future possible, but the arts help us enjoy that future. So read some poetry. Get lost in a great novel. Go to a museum or to see an orchestra perform. What's life without appreciating its beauty?

7. Do things that have no relevance whatsoever to your STEM future. We're all for STEM (hey, we wrote a book about it!), but all work and no play can make you not only dull but super stressed out, too! Set aside some time to do things just for fun, even if they won't necessarily get you into Harvard.

8. Take care of the planet. Whether your interest is in earth science, geology, zoology, or a related earth-friendly field, we can all do our part to take care of this awesome planet we call home. So plant a tree, clean up some roadside garbage, or find other ways to get involved with conservation.

9. Consider playing a sport. Many of the women we interviewed for this book mentioned how sports teams helped them learn about working with others and staying focused. You don't necessarily have to think of sports as a distraction from your studies—they might improve them!

10. Take tech breaks. While we all love technology, you can get too much of a good thing. Take a walk outside once in a while and breathe some fresh air. At least occasionally, trade in *pew pew!* for birds singing *tweet tweet!*

11. Make friends with failure. One of the greatest things we learned from the women in this book? Failure is not fatal. It can be a fantastic learning experience . . . and it can make you a much stronger person and build your character! When you fall down, get back up.

12. Accept free money. Sure, it sounds like a no-brainer, but you'd be surprised how many schools and organizations are just dying to give you scholarships or stipends for studying STEM. If there's something you want to do but

don't have the funds, do some research. You'll probably find a group willing to help you.

13. Learn how to code. Computers aren't going away anytime soon, so it wouldn't hurt to know how to make them do what they do. Coding skills can only benefit you in whatever field you choose.

14. Play with your STEM. Math and the analytical skills involved in science and technology don't have to be a chore. Choose puzzles and games that will sharpen your skills. (You can even become your family's "human calculator" and make a game of adding up real-life numbers in your head, just like Tiera did as a kid!)

15. Learn a trade. Many schools offer classes in cool subjects such as welding and carpentry, which can lead to outstanding careers in and of themselves or just increase your knowledge of how things work and are made. Or you can build your skills—and a house!—by volunteering with Habitat for Humanity or similar organizations.

16. Invent something! Got a great idea? The world could probably use it. You can do a patent search at http://uspto.gov/patft to see if your idea is original enough to consider getting your very own patent to protect it.

SUGGESTIONS FOR FURTHER READING

FOR MORE INSPIRING STORIES OF WOMEN IN STEM, CHECK OUT:

Acevedo, Sylvia. *Path to the Stars: My Journey from Girl Scout to Rocket Scientist.* Boston: Houghton Mifflin Harcourt, 2018.

Holt, Nathalia. *Rise of the Rocket Girls: The Women Who Propelled Us, from Missiles to the Moon to Mars.* New York: Back Bay Books, 2017.

Ignotofsky, Rachel. *Women in Science: 50 Fearless Pioneers Who Changed the World.* Berkeley, CA: Ten Speed Press, 2016.

Montgomery, Sy. *Temple Grandin: How the Girl Who Loved Cows Embraced Autism and Changed the World.* Boston: Houghton Mifflin Harcourt, 2014.

O'Connell, Caitlin, and Donna M. Jackson. *The Elephant Scientist.* Boston: Houghton Mifflin Books for Children,

2011. (And other books in the Scientists in the Field series.)

Shetterly, Margot Lee. *Hidden Figures (Young Readers' Edition).* New York: HarperCollins, 2016.

Stone, Tanya Lee. *Almost Astronauts: 13 Women Who Dared to Dream.* Somerville, MA: Candlewick Press, 2009.

Thimmesh, Catherine. *Girls Think of Everything: Stories of Ingenious Inventions by Women.* Boston: Houghton Mifflin Harcourt, 2002.

TO LEARN MORE ABOUT STEM SUBJECTS, CHECK OUT:

Benjamin, Arthur, and Michael Shermer. *Secrets of Mental Math: The Mathemagician's Guide to Lightning Calculation and Amazing Math Tricks.* New York: Three Rivers Press, 2006.

Betts, Bruce. *Astronomy for Kids: How to Explore Outer Space with Binoculars, a Telescope, or Just Your Eyes!* Emeryville, CA: Rockridge Press, 2018.

Carter, Rita, et al. *The Human Brain Book.* New York: DK, 2019.

Cate, Annette LeBlanc. *Look Up!: Bird-Watching in Your Own Backyard.* Somerville, MA: Candlewick Press, 2013.

Challoner, Jack. *Smithsonian: STEM Lab.* New York: DK Children, 2019.

Cham, Jorge, and Daniel Whiteson. *We Have No Idea: A Guide to the Unknown Universe.* New York: Riverhead Books, 2017.

Chatterton, Crystal. *Awesome Science Experiments for Kids: 100+ Fun STEAM Projects & Why They Work.* Emeryville, CA: Rockridge Press, 2018.

Ignotofsky, Rachel. *The Wondrous Workings of Planet Earth: Understanding Our World and Its Ecosystems.* New York: Ten Speed Press, 2018.

LEGO Gadgets. New York: Klutz, 2018.

Munroe, Randall. *Thing Explainer: Complicated Stuff in Simple Words.* Boston: Houghton Mifflin Harcourt, 2015.

Young Rewired State. *Get Coding! Learn HTML, CSS, and JavaScript and Build a Website, App, and Game.* Somerville, MA: Candlewick Press, 2017.

PHOTO CREDITS

Except where noted below, the photographs of the scientists were provided courtesy of the individual scientists.

pp. ii–iii, viii–ix, 135–145, 196–197: Image of handwritten mathematical formulas courtesy of Shutterstock/Marina Sun

pp. iv–v, 67–77: Image of 3D frame tunnel courtesy of Shutterstock/Irina1 Melnik

pp. iv–v, 79–89, 188: Image of sea depth topographic map courtesy of Shutterstock/Alex Gontar

pp. vi–vii, 7–19, 176–180: Image of mathematical integral formulas courtesy of Shutterstock/Sashkin

pp. vi–vii, 37–51, 185–187: Image of vector binary code courtesy of Shutterstock/luzvykova Iaroslava

pp. viii–ix, 1–5, 175: Image of engineering blueprint courtesy of Shutterstock/Bubushonok

pp. 21–35, 181–184: Image of neurons in the brain courtesy of Shutterstock/Rost9

p. 63: Image of tapir courtesy of Shutterstock/Milan Rybar

p. 69: Image of Dr. Newman in the BioSuit copyright © Joshua Dalsimer

p. 82: Image of the *JOIDES Resolution* courtesy of the Integrated Ocean Drilling Program U.S. Implementing Organization (IODP USIO)/William Crawford

pp. 91–103: Image of particle fission fractal courtesy of Shutterstock/sakkmesterke

pp. 105–119, 189–195: Image of *Staphylococcus aureus* courtesy of Shutterstock/Microspectacular

p. 119: Image of *Mir* courtesy of NASA

pp. 121–133, 174: Image of skin cells courtesy of Shutterstock/nobeastsofierce

p. 142: Image of starshade copyright © NASA/JPL-Caltech

pp. 147–157: Image of embryos courtesy of Shutterstock/BioFoto

pp. 159–173: Image of rainbow mosaic courtesy of Shutterstock/tuulijumala

p. 160: Image of Lexus copyright © Toyota Motor Sales, U.S.A., Inc.

INDEX

bone marrow, 133
brain surgery, 22, 34
Brazil, 53, 55
Brown University, 79
bullying, 84, 126, 129
butterflies, 160–161, 163, 167,
    170–173

camps, 100, 130, 181
cancer, 148–149, 153, 156
carbon dioxide emissions, 81,
    86–87, 88–89
career choices, 2, 8, 15, 27, 58,
    166
career fairs, 58
cars. *See* automobiles
celerity, 103
certified public accountants, 39
chemicals, 106, 108
chemistry, 139, 153
China, 162–165
civil rights, 93
climate change, 80–81, 88
climate models, 80
clubs, 182
college
    admissions, 27–28, 57, 58
    choosing, 25–26
    graduate degrees, 28, 96,
        127–128, 165
    majors, 26–27, 44, 72, 95
    paying for, 57, 59, 72, 112,
        113
    study abroad, 164, 165
colors, 161–163, 170
Columbia University, 79, 85
comfort zone, 32, 182
compression wear, 75
computer games, 37. *See also*
    video games

computer programming, 40–41,
    50–51, 142
computer science engineers, 38
Cornell University, 21, 25–26
cosmos, 136
Cousteau, Jacques, 83
creativity, 73, 87, 168

dabbling, 46
designers, 49, 50
difficult projects, 47–48
diffraction, 172
disappointments, 29
discoveries, 153–154
diseases
    in animals, 30, 31
    cancer, 148–149, 153, 156
    infections, 123, 131
    researching, 18, 34, 37–38
diversity, 16, 111, 113, 165
doctors, 21, 28, 34, 148, 153
DOS (disk operating system), 41
dreams, 5, 73, 86, 169
drillships, 79–80, 82, 83
Durgana, Davina, 7–17

Earth
    history of, 80–82
    saving, 88–89, 183
Einstein, Albert, 103
El Salvador, 12
electromagnetic spectrum, 97,
    161
Endocrinology (journal), 147
engineering
    aerospace, 2–3, 67, 72
    biomedical, 124
    forestry engineers, 59
    and immunology, 122, 124,
        128

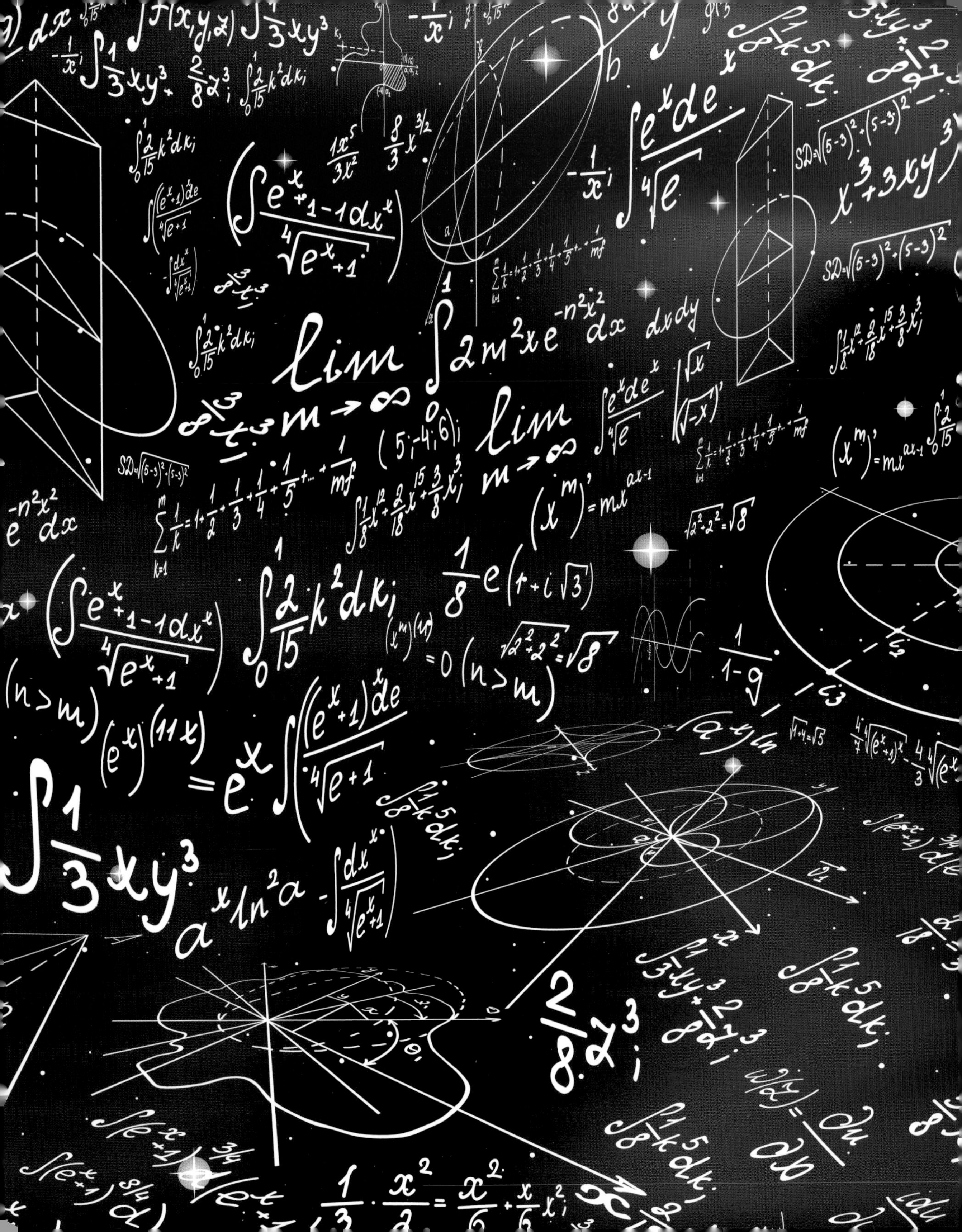